THE
MISSISSIPPI RIVER

First English edition published by Colour Library Books Ltd.
© 1984 Illustrations and text: Colour Library Books Ltd.,
  Guildford, Surrey, England.
This edition published by Crescent Books
Distributed by Crown Publishers, Inc.
h g f e d c b a
Display and text filmsetting by Acesetters Ltd.,
  Richmond, Surrey, England.
Color separations by Llovet, Barcelona, Spain.
Printed and bound in Barcelona, Spain.
by JISA-RIEUSSET and EUROBINDER.
ISBN 0 517 429489
CRESCENT 1984

THE MISSISSIPPI RIVER

text by
ANN Mc CARTHY

Featuring the photography of
JULIAN ESSAM

Produced by
TED SMART and DAVID GIBBON

CRESCENT BOOKS
NEW YORK

Before the coming of the white man the Mississippi River was a catalyst for a diversified Indian population. They had lived along its banks for countless generations.

For the most part, they farmed and lived peacefully in permanent villages between their fields and the river. That the Mississippi might be marketable was inconceivable to the Indians. The river was just there. To call it their own made no more sense than to stake a claim to the forests, mountains or sky. As Indians they revered the spirit of the mighty river, for such a great natural force would surely have a powerful spirit. The river could be an enraged enemy, or a trusted friend, but was always comforting as a familiar presence. Above all, the river provided food and a means of transportation. It also provided passage to the restless white man who would eventually destroy the Indian's way of life.

Sixteenth and seventeenth-century European explorers had varying expectations from the vast American wilderness. The French persisted as long as they could in the belief that this nation was only a minor barrier on the trade route to China, sending one thwarted expedition after another to find a passage through this piece of land. At last they accepted the limited boundaries of the nearly empty American continent.

The Spaniards, more than all other peoples, were disillusioned in North America. Because of their successful search for gold in Mexico and Peru, they arrived in America swollen with riches, arrogance and anticipation of finding further wealth. Narvez, Coronado and then de Soto plundered through the wilderness. Wearing silks and satins, the adventurers stumbled through swamp and forest with their ineffective armies and impractical armor. They were beset by fever, hunger, violent storms, cold, dysentery, hostile Indians and death.

In 1532 Hernando de Soto returned to Spain from Peru loaded down with gold and puffed with inflated feelings of glory.

Seven years later he landed at the present-day site of Tampa, Florida. An epoch of exploitation, savagery and futility was to follow. De Soto claimed Florida for Spain and then led his band into the North American continent, eager to put to use his skills as a conqueror of Indians.

However, these Indians were not what he expected. They were too unsophisticated to venerate his evident superiority; too barbaric to know the rules of civilized warfare. They caught de Soto and his men off guard by suddenly appearing from behind bushes. Because of a stubborn belief in the inferiority of their enemy, the Spanish never mastered the methods of guerilla warfare: nor could they defend against it.

The Indians were friendly at first but no friendships endured. The white men slaughtered and enslaved with casual cruelty. They took food, valuables and women and they used the men as carriers. The Indians soon learned that they could rid themselves of the invaders by inventing tales of great treasures possessed by faraway tribes. Consequently, the Spanish conquistadores pursued erratic routes on their quest for gold, fighting all along the way. Then, in the spring of 1541, twenty-three months after they had landed in Florida, de Soto and his companions met the Mississippi.

It was a muddy, dangerous, two-mile-wide obstacle which they gladly left behind in their continuing pursuit of the "golden city." The following winter showed them no mercy. Two hundred and fifty men had died. They were bitterly cold, filled with despair and unable to escape by the perilous river. On May 21, 1542, de Soto succumbed to a fever. To conceal his mortality from the Indians, he was placed in a hollow log and dropped into the river he had discovered.

It would be more than a century before the wilderness along the Mississippi would again be infested with inquisitive, self-seeking and courageous foreigners. The men of Western Europe continued to be challenged by the idea of conquering the New World, its great river and the sea that should lead to China. From the first, the

French showed themselves to be more suited to an untamed life. They possessed seafaring skills, patience and endurance. With an enlightened understanding of the new country, Samuel de Champlain established his colony on the rock of Quebec. The Jesuits followed him with an intense fervor for their spiritual mission.

In 1634 Champlain sent Jean Nicolet on a voyage of exploration. Guided by seven Indians he journeyed up the Ottawa River, through the Lakes to Green Bay in Michigan and eventually to the Fox River. It was the farthest northwestern point yet to be reached by a white man. As he searched for the access to China he encountered Winnebago Indians who thought he was the god of thunder when they heard him fire his gun.

Nicolet carried a brightly-colored damask gown with a flower and bird design, so he would be properly attired when he met the Chinese. However, feeling that his mission was accomplished when he neared the supposed Sea of China, he turned back.

And so, a new assemblage of priests and traders set out to penetrate the wilds.

The Sioux Indians told Chouart Groseilliers and Pierre Radisson, two traders who spent the winter of 1658 to 1659 on the south shores of Lake Superior, of the existence of a river "of huge extent." Jesuit priest Father Allouez named this still unseen river "Missipi." Finally, on June 17, 1673, Father Jacques Marquette and fur-trader Louis Joliet entered the Mississippi from the Wisconsin River. The two dauntless explorers, one in search of souls to save, and one in search of trading supremacy, traveled by canoe as far south as the Arkansas. Their sole permit for moving amidst the Indian tribes was a calumet, or peace pipe, which saved their lives on numerous occasions. Marquette and Joliet permanently put to rest the inaccurate report that the Mississippi flowed west to the Gulf of California and eventually to China. They hurried to Quebec to tell the French intendant that the Mississippi emptied into the Gulf of Mexico but couldn't finish what they had begun because Louis Count de Frontenac chose René Robert Cavelier, sieur de la Salle to develop the Mississippi basin.

La Salle's attitude toward the New World was realistic. His vision deviated from that of his adventurous predecessors who viewed America as a source of temporary treasures and the Mississippi as a means to another continent. La Salle recognized what the river would mean to France. He requested finance for an expedition of large boats to navigate the river and for the establishment of permanent trading posts. He received the funds along with a right to bear arms, designated as a black shield embossed with a running greyhound in silver and an eight-point star in gold. La Salle's family, prosperous wool-traders from Rouen, gave him money for fur-trading at Fort Frontenac on the upper Saint Lawrence.

But La Salle couldn't be dissuaded from his dream of acquiring the Mississippi for France. In 1680 he built Fort Crevecoeur on Lake Peoria as a first step towards achieving that goal. Sadly, that fort was destroyed by a mutinous garrison of men who abandoned La Salle, undermining five years of his life. Still, he and his loyal lieutenant, Henry de Tonti, led fifty men on an expedition down the lower Mississippi in the spring of 1682. They arrived at the river's confluence with the sea on April 9, planted the standard of royal France, and La Salle proclaimed, "In the name of the most high, mighty, invincible, and victorious Prince Louis the Great...I...do take possession of this country...the seas, harbors, ports, bays, adjacent straits; and all the nations, people, provinces, cities, towns, villages, mines, minerals, fisheries, streams, rivers..."

He called the vast domain Louisiana in honor of King Louis XIV.

La Salle had begun his exploration on the upper Mississippi, but knew the value of the lower river. "We should obtain everything which has enriched New England and Virginia...timber of every kind, salted meat, tallow, corn, sugar, tobacco, honey, wax, resin, and other gums...immense pasturages...a prodigious number of buffaloes, stags, hinds, roes, bears, otters, lynxes...hides and furs...there are cotton, cochineal nuts, turn-soles...entire forests of mulberry trees...slate, coal, vines, apple-trees..." La Salle intended to control the resources of his expansive empire by building forts and establishing colonies in the Illinois region and at the mouth of the Mississippi. He received official permission to pursue his plans and, in 1684, La Salle, Tonti, 400 men and four ships sailed from France to the New World. The journey was filled with disaster; first the naval commander refused to obey La Salle, then Spanish pirates captured one of the ships, crew members deserted, and La Salle contracted a long illness. After all that, he and his diminished crew of 180 missed the mouth of the Mississippi and disembarked four hundred miles to the west. La Salle had lost his river. He and a portion of his less than 45 remaining men made a fruitless attempt to reach Canada where they could get help.

In January, 1687, exhausted and starving, half of the survivors set out for a last time. The search was blighted; La Salle was assassinated by one of his own men.

French control of the Mississippi River ended in 1763 at the close of the French and Indian War. The Great War for the Empire began over the specific issue of the upper Ohio Valley. Both Britain and France claimed it as part of their Empire. They each desired to dominate the heart of the continent of North America and a conflict concerning territorial claims was inevitable. At the Peace Treaty of 1763 in Paris, France relinquished Canada and land east of the Mississippi to England; Spain lost Florida but gained Louisiana, including New Orleans. The entire Atlantic seaboard belonged to Britain.

The Americans, understandably, were displeased with Britain's dominion and rebelled in 1775. The Mississippi River was an important battle zone during the American Revolution; without it there was no access to New Orleans, a supply base for American forces in the West. A critical expedition under the command of George Rogers Clark moved on the upper Mississippi. France and Spain entered the war on the American side, so tactical areas of the river were dominated by people sympathetic to the American cause.

The British were unable to repossess the region from Clark and after the Treaty of Paris in 1783, which ended the long war, the United States controlled all of the Mississippi's east bank except the Isle of Orleans at its mouth.

Spain owned that island and the city of New Orleans until 1800, when King Charles IV of Spain ceded Louisiana back to France. That transaction included the significant port of New Orleans, the strategic mouth of the Mississippi River and much of the area between the Mississippi and the Rocky Mountains. Obviously, the subsistence of westward moving settlers depended upon their unrestrained use of the Mississippi and the port of New Orleans.

Robert R. Livingston, President Jefferson's emissary to France, with the assistance of James Monroe, purchased not only New Orleans, but all of the Louisiana territory. Napoleon's asking price was $15 million and, in May of 1803, Livingston and Monroe signed the treaty for the Louisiana Purchase.

The stage was set for further expansion. Jefferson immediately dispatched an expedition under Meriwether Lewis and William Clark to explore the region. The journey of Lewis and Clark up the Missouri River and down the Columbia to the Pacific Ocean provided priceless geographical information resulting in an American claim to Oregon and the Western coast.

Now that both sides of the Mississippi were American, the full development of its waterway could proceed. The Ohio Valley was filled with farmers who found trade outlets to the East far too restrictive. The only way that they and farmers from other areas could efficiently move their produce was by floating it down the Mississippi in either flatboats or keelboats.

Birch or elm bark canoes, hollowed-out trunks of trees called pirogues, a variety of flat-bottomed bateaux, all came down the river. But the flatboat and keelboat carried cargo. The flatboats, called Kentucky boats, were one-way, downstream arks with shelters for the men, places for cooking fires, quarters for livestock, and storage for cargo. The boats could be 60 feet long and 20 feet wide. Men rowed the boats, but when the wind blew upstream, or the boat grounded on a sand bar, or snagged a sawyer (a floating tree attached by its roots to the river bottom), the flatboatmen needed extra strength.

The flatboats unloaded their freight in the down-river towns, then were torn apart and sold for lumber. After partying, the flatboatmen started back up north and east, mostly on foot.

The keelboat, similar in size to its competitor, had a roof to protect cargo and passengers, and the ability to go back up-river against the current.

The men who carried the river's commerce before the steamboat were superhuman: "half horse and half alligator." The downriver trip, by keelboat, was easy enough; they had only to keep in the current and, occasionally, push the boat off a sand bar. Free to drink, play cards, fish, shoot, sing, dance juba and misbehave, they were a continual source of disquiet for rivertown settlers. Their force was felt when they roared into a community; people protected their womenfolk, especially.

Natchez-under-the-Hill was the keelboatman's kind of town. There the bawdy roustabouts usually rollicked all evening. The next day they would head south again, destined for New Orleans, where the goods would be dropped off.

The journey upstream was a harsh contrast. The continuous struggle against the current was relieved only at those rare times when the wind was from the right quarter and a sail could be used. It took three to four months to go from New Orleans to the trading towns at the head of the Ohio River. For each man in the crew there were three thousand pounds of cargo. When the banks were open enough, the crew pulled the boat upstream by a rope called the cordelle, which was fastened to the mast. Twenty or more men attached themselves to the rope and heaved, stumbling through mud, sand and rocks. In shallow water they poled the boat, or they bushwhacked, using branches and young trees on the shore to move slowly along. The three oars on each side were used only during occasional stretches of quiet water.

Skillful maneuvering was required when ascending the rapids, the most treacherous and arduous part of the trip. None but the brave and brawny enlisted in the keelboating service. As they sweated under the burning sun, stripped to the waist, they acquired extraordinary toughness. At night they gulped their rations of whiskey, half-burnt meat and half-baked bread, and then plunked down on the deck to sleep.

The cocky boatmen dressed in scarlet shirts and bright blue jackets when they went to town. The king of these men was Mike Fink, a hero, like Daniel Boone and Davy Crockett, who could outswear, outfight, outdrink, outshoot, outdance, outsing all other "river giants".

Mike Fink really lived, though many of the stories about him are legend. He died in 1822 and the method of his demise is debated. The following tale is as likely as any:

"For Mike Fink a joke was a joke, and no opportunity should be missed for a laugh. It was the crude but accepted code of his calling.

"'So yer th' best gunshot on the river, Mike Fink,' a fellow keelboatman had taunted him, as the group frolicked on a sand bar at nightfall, somewhere along the tortuous way up the Mississippi.

"'Well, then, prove yer my friend fer life,' continued Mike's taunter. The strenuous, inch by inch poling of the heavy craft against the current developed mighty muscles on these men of iron, and it also developed the will to play hard when evening came. But friendship was something stronger than muscle among them, and friendships, by a strange quirk of reasoning, had to be proved.

"'I'll prove it, and these hands that can t'ar a hide off a buffalo, can shoot an apple off yer head.' Marksmanship was Mike Fink's long suit.

"As the smoke fron the smudge fire rose lazily into the twilight, Mike placed a red-ripe apple on his taunter's noggin.

"...They had fought like beasts, these two had, but that was past. Now they were fast friends and Mike was going to prove it. He backed away, turned, and smiled. Then he paced off forty giant strides. He liftd his rifle, aimed, smiled again – and fired. All eyes saw the man pitch forward to the moist sand. The apple fell unharmed to his side.

"'Bang!'

"The pistol of the man's younger brother cracked the stillness again, and Mike Fink staggered slowly, trying to support himself on his gun until he, too, sank to the sand.

"But nobody was looking at Mike. They were looking at the man who had the apple shot off his head, Mike's pal, who had suddenly gained his feet, as if risen from the dead, and was stumbling toward Mike in astonishment.

"The young man, believing that Mike had killed from pure wantonness, had avenged his brother. What Mike had done was merely to displace the apple by shooting between it and his friend's skull. Not even blood had been drawn.

"That took marksmanship. It also took Mike's life."

But other keelboatmen lived to transport the rivertowns' produce. In 1821 New Orleans received 52,750 tons of cargo by flatboats, barges and keelboats and 54,120 by steamboats. Though all the craft carried the first major commerce, moving lumber, corn, tobacco, wheat, and furs downstream to the delta country; and sugar, molasses, cotton and whiskey, north, steamboats gradually became dominant.

"Keelboating died a permanent death" according to Mark Twain. "The keelboatman became a deck-hand, or a mate, or a pilot on a steamer; and when steamer-berths were not open to him, he took a berth on a Pittsburg coal-flat, or on a pine raft constructed in the forests up toward the sources of the Mississippi." Twain remembers the "rude ways and tremendous talk of...the ex-keelman and their admiringly patterning successors" which he describes in *The Adventures of Huckleberry Finn*.

"...You know a young person can't wait very well when he is impatient to find out a thing. We talked it over, and by and by Jim said it was such a black night, now, that it wouldn't be no risk to swim down to the big raft and crawl aboard and listen – they would talk about Cairo.
"...So I swum down along the raft till I was 'most abreast the camp fire in the middle, then I crawled aboard and inched along and got in among some bundles of shingles on the weather side of the fire. There was thirteen men there – they was the watch on deck of course. And a mighty rough-looking lot, too. They had a jug, and tin cups, and they kept the jug moving. One man was singing – roaring, you may say; and it wasn't a nice song – for a parlor, anyway. He roared through his nose, and strung out the last word of every line very long. When he was done they all fetched a kind of Injun war-whoop, and another was sung. It begun:

"'There was a woman in our towdn,
   In our towdn did dwed'l [dwell],
   She loved her husband dear-i-lee,
   But another man twyste as wed'l.
   'Singing too, riloo, riloo, riloo,
       Ri-too, riloo, rilay—e,
   She loved her husband dear-i-lee,
   But another man twyste as wed'l.'

"And so on – fourteen verses. It was kind of poor, and when he was going to start on the next verse one of them said it was the tune the old cow died on; and another said: 'Oh, give a rest!' And another one told him to take a walk. They made fun of him till he got mad and jumped up and began to cuss the crowd, and said he could lam any thief in the lot.
"They was all about to make a break for him when the biggest man jumped up and says:
"'Set whar you are, gentlemen. Leave him to me; he's my meat.'
"Then he jumped up in the air three times, and cracked his heels together every time. He flung off a buckskin coat that was all hung with fringes, and says, 'You lay thar tell the chawin-up's done;' and flung his hat down, which was all over ribbons, and says, 'You lay thar tell his sufferin's over.'
"Then he jumped up in the air and cracked his heels together again, and shouted:
"'Whoo-oop! I'm the old original iron-jawed, brass-mounted, copper-bellied corpse-maker from the wilds of Arkansaw! Look at me! I'm the man they call Sudden Death and General Desolation! Sired by a hurricane, dam'd by an earthquake, half-brother to the cholera, nearly related to the small-pox on my mother's side! Look at me! I take nine alligators and a bar'l of whiskey for breakfast when I'm in robust health, and a bushel of rattlesnakes and a dead body when I'm ailing. I split the everlasting rocks with my glance, and I squench the thunder when I speak! Whoo-oop! Stand back and give me room according to my strength! Blood's my natural drink, and the wails of the dying is music to my ear! Cast your eye on me, Gentlemen! And lay low and hold your breath, for I'm 'bout to turn myself loose!'
"The original challenger responded to that barrage with equal bravado, but they were all talk and no show. As they was edging away in different directions ...a little black-whiskered chap grabbed the chicken-livered cowards and thrashed them."

The man who became known as Mark Twain was born Samuel Langhorne Clemens in 1835. From the beginning, his heart belonged to the Mississippi. He grew up in Hannibal, Missouri, and like most rivertown youngsters, he longed to be a steamboat pilot. The pilot was revered above all others. He was the king of the river. Sam Clemens became a cub pilot on a steamboat in 1857, but his mentor fell short of being kingly, causing young Sam to say, "It seemed to me that I had put my life in the keeping of a peculiarly reckless outcast." In truth young Sam thought that Mr. Bixby, his captain, was infallible. He relates one of the first times he had "sole charge" of the boat. Mr. Bixby had gone below for a short time, but not short enough. "I vaingloriously turned my back and inspected the stern marks and hummed a tune, a sort of easy indifference which I had prodigiously admired in Bixby and other great pilots. Once I had inspected too long and, when I faced to the front again my heart flew into my mouth so suddenly that if I hadn't clapped my teeth together I should have lost it." A crash on a frightful bluff was imminent. To no avail, Sam implemented every resource in his repertoire, which was difficult for a boy who was so terrified that he "didn't know which end he stood on." And then Mr. Bixby calmly stepped on to the hurricane deck and Sam's terror subsided. "I would have felt safe on the brink of Niagara with Mr. Bixby on the hurricane deck." Still, learning to be a cub pilot was a grueling experience, especially for someone whose "memory was never loaded with anything but blank cartridges."

Sam continues "At the end of what seemed a tedious while, I had managed to pack my head full of islands, towns, bars, 'points', and bends; and a curiously inanimate mass of lumber it was, too. However, inasmuch as I could shut my eyes and reel off a good long string of these names without leaving out more than ten miles of river in every fifty, I began to feel that I could make her skip those little gaps. But of course my complacency could hardly get start enough to lift my nose a trifle into the air, before Mr. Bixby would think of something to fetch it down again. One day he turned on me suddenly with this settler:

"'What is the shape of Walnut Bend?'
"He might as well have asked me my grandmother's opinion of protoplasm. I reflected respectfully, and then said I didn't know it had any particular shape. My gunpowdery chief went off with a bang, of course, and then went on loading and firing until he was out of adjectives.
"I learned long ago that he only carried just so many rounds of ammunition, and was sure to subside into a very placable and even remorseful old smooth-bore as soon as they were all gone. That word 'old' is merely affectionate; he was not more than thirty-four. I waited. By and by he said:
"'My boy, you've got to know the shape of the river perfectly. It is all there is left to steer by on a very dark night. Everything else is blotted out and gone. But mind

you, it hasn't the same shape in the night that it has in the daytime.'
"'You only learn the shape of the river; and you learn it with such absolute certainty that you can always steer by the shape that's in your head, and never mind the one that's before your eyes."

Mark Twain did learn the river. "The face of the water, in time became a wonderful book – a book that was a dead language to the uneducated passenger, but which told its mind to me without reserve..."

Though Mark Twain's painstaking pursuit and acquisition of knowledge diminished the river's romance for him, he was never happier than when piloting a boat on his beloved Mississippi. However, Twain was a relative Johnny-come-lately when it came to steamboats.

The first steamboat to ply the Mississippi River was launched at Pittsburg in 1811 and piloted to New Orleans by Nicholas Roosevelt, an ancestor of Theodore. The circumstances behind that historic voyage began at a farm on the Hudson River where Nicholas Roosevelt, between chores, built a model boat with paddle wheels turned by an axle cord attached to springs of hickory and whalebone. A few years later in Philadelphia he met his future father-in-law, Benjamin Henry Latrobe, an engineer and architect. While Latrobe was working on a municipal water system, Roosevelt constructed steam engines. During that time, Lydia Latrobe, who frequently visited her father, attracted the attention of Roosevelt.

Meanwhile, in France, Chancellor Robert R. Livingston, the man who negotiated the Louisiana Purchase for Jefferson, was experimenting with steam navigation. He and artist/inventor Robert Fulton embarked a ship on the Seine, but they didn't impress either the French or English Ministries. So Fulton returned to America and, with funds supplied by Livingston, built the steam-propelled Clermont and took it up the Hudson from New York to Albany.

As a result of that accomplishment Livingston and Fulton sought, in the Eastern states and in Washington, D.C., a series of patents and charters that would give them exclusive rights to carry on steam navigation for a period of years. Only Louisiana granted the eastern capitalists a monopoly charter, and that grant included New Orleans.

The sole privilege of New Orleans' port meant control of the West's commerce. Plans to navigate the Mississippi by steam began immediately and that's when Nicholas Roosevelt came in.

Nicholas Roosevelt married Lydia Latrobe and, despite the protests of family and friends, ventured into an unorthodox honeymoon. They traveled down the Mississippi on a flatboat, charting the river's flow, depth and deterrents for a steamboat. Though Roosevelt made the journey as pleasant as possible, installing a bedroom, kitchen and dining room, and engaging a pilot, cook and three boatmen, the adventure wasn't without peril. The exposed craft met with cantankerous weather, and the fear of conflict with unfriendly natives continually hounded them.

However, the junket was a success. Roosevelt determined that a steamboat could travel the western rivers despite the hazards of sand bars, snags, sawyers and shifting channels.

Roosevelt, Livingston and Fulton formed the Ohio Steamboat Navigation Company and hired builders from New York to construct the *New Orleans* at a shipyard in Pittsburg. Starting from the East, Roosevelt and his young, pregnant wife set off for the Mississippi in September, 1811. The gray-blue, two-masted side-wheeler *New Orleans* received enthusiastic acclaim as she traveled downstream, but skeptics were certain that the craft would never make it upstream. To quell the skepticism Roosevelt invited a number of guests on board, at Louisville. While they were dining, the steamboat backed away from the landing and successfully moved against the current. On another occasion, Roosevelt proudly steamed the side-wheeler to Cincinnati and back to Louisville. While at anchor a short distance below the Ohio Falls at Louisville the *New Orleans* became caught in the cataclysm of the New Madrid earthquake. The violent tremors endangered the lives of everyone aboard. After the river's torment subsided the steamboat continued her maiden voyage, but the course, so carefully charted by the pioneer pilot, was dramatically altered by the earthquake. When the steamboat eventually reached Natchez, the citizens shouted welcomes to the side-wheeler and its passengers and then watched Roosevelt accept the first steamboat cargo on the Mississippi. Cotton was consigned to New Orleans and delivered there on January 12, 1812. For two years the *New Orleans* was the sole transporter of cotton and supplies from Natchez to New Orleans, and then Henry Miller Shreve broke the monopoly.

The War of 1812 delayed the impact of the steamboat on the river more than the previous year's earthquake. Shreve formed a partnership with Daniel French and the company built the 75-ton steamboat *Enterprise*. By the time Captain Shreve arrived in New Orleans, however, the city was beleaguered by British troops.

Shreve gladly complied with General Andrew Jackson's command to press the *Enterprise* into service for the transport of troops and supplies.

The American economy stagnated during the war. The entire country east of the Mississippi was largely involved in the fighting, which was for the most part directed against the pro-British Indian population. Great Britain, occupied with Napoleon until mid-1814, waited until then to wage its major offense aagainst the Americans. The British knew that if they could seize control of New Orleans and the lower Mississippi, they could economically cripple the interior of the United States. They most likely suspected that the predominately French population of Louisiana would then give their allegiance to Britain, who sustained a strong interest in the fur trade of the Southeast and the upper Mississippi Valley.

Because the Treaty of Ghent had been signed, the outcome of the Battle of New Orleans was academic. Still, the story of that battle is remembered. Sir Edward Packenham and 7,500 British regulars mounted the attack on January 8, 1815.

Andrew Jackson and his troops, numbering about six or seven thousand, were waiting silently for them behind cotton bales. When the British army emerged from the morning mist, the Americans had heard the skirl of bagpipes and the beat of drums long before they saw the soldiers. Jackson's men held their fire until the British, in their traditional bright red coats, were virtually on top of them. The battle lasted only half an hour and ended in total victory for the Americans. Andrew

Jackson became a full-fledged hero and the Mississippi River entered a forty-five-year period of transportation prominence.

It was Henry M. Shreve who, in 1816, came up with the first vessel which would truly meet the requirements of the Mississippi. The four-hundred-ton *Washington* established a pattern for future steamboats. The boiler was moved out of the hold, beginning the precedent of all machinery being placed above the water line. This allowed the boats to be built with the extremely shallow draft necessary to navigate the sand-bar-filled western rivers. Cargo decks, boiler decks and passenger decks were stacked above the water-line, giving the impression of a floating layer cake.

Though slightly daunted by the panic of 1819, the next forty years of Mississippi River history would be dominated by the steamboat. One man reports that he is grateful for this phenomenon.

The crew and officers of a tinseled river steamer noticed one day that one of the passengers did not get off. For nearly a month he traveled up and down the Mississippi without setting foot on dry land. He wasn't a gambler, a thief or a murderer; in fact, he was unusually gregarious, offering cigars, buying toddies, chatting with the rest of the passengers. Nevertheless, everyone was curious. Finally the captain questioned the man about his ineffable behavior.

The response has become historic: "Of course, sir, I'll tell you. It's the finest way to pleasure myself that I know. No hotel in America can equal this. The finest food – your wild game, your glazed fish, your roasts, sauces and pastry! My cabin is as finely-equipped, as well-decorated, as any room I've enjoyed in my life. The bar, the cabin, the promenade – nothing to match 'em, I tell you. And the company! I meet all my friends, the best people in the world. Why should I want to leave?" And everybody agreed the man was right.

Splendor on the river came in the form of a steamboat. The outer design varied little, but the individual interiors, though always lavish, had distinct personalities. Still, there were certain invariables. The walls and ceilings of the enormously long cabins were of ornately-carved wood; lush patterned carpet covered the floor; elegant chandeliers hung from the ceiling; a

piano sat at one end of the room; and velvet-covered chairs lined the walls. Oil paintings, statues, and mirrors reflecting lovely images augmented the opulence. In the huge dining rooms, tables stretched so far that those at one end could barely recognise friends at the other; and between them rose mountains of food, garlands of flowers, multi-colored ices and desserts in designs that "the lady passengers tried to imitate at home."

There were barrooms, barber shops, saloons, women's cabins, private suites and private rooms for card games. Stateroom doors were decorated with hand-painted floral patterns. In addition a number of captains offered bridal suites with pink and blue cupids covering the walls. According to a contemporary account, "the planters talked crops over their gin fizzes; children ran up and down the white stairways under the eyes of governesses; matrons folded their hands and kept a hawk's view over the behavior of all who passed before them, while their sons and daughters strolled arm in arm about the decks."

Food was an important part of steamboat experience. Passengers became connoisseurs during the adventure, or at least big eaters. There were no restrictions on the servings of smothered robins, duck en gelée or blancmange with spiced peaches, and waiters presented the epicurean dishes with flair. On shore the waiters offered polished fruit, frozen creams, and rare confections to lovely ladies and the wives of prestigious planters.

As the boats became more palatial and the captains more pretentious, races between them became more heated. However, the greatest steamboat competition of all didn't happen until 1870, when the *Natchez* raced the *Robert E. Lee.*

The splendor of the steamboat was matched by the supremacy of its captain. He was "lord, tyrant, temperamental monarch, a man of gracious favor for those he liked, of thundering contempt for those he disliked." Tom Leathers, Master of the *Natchez*, epitomized the steamboat captain. He was nearly six feet four and weighed two hundred and seventy pounds. His locks and curling white mustache stayed in place to the last hair, and his costume was all fine whites with white hat or blacks with black hat. He carried a cigar almost as if it were a baton, and his blue eyes rapidly changed from smiling agreement to raging command.

Captain Tom had a manner with ladies and powerful plantation owners that was so courtly it seemed a caricature, but among roustabouts and crew members, he was praised as the "best curser on the Mississippi."

Captain John W. Cannon, like Tom Leathers, was a Kentuckian. Cannon captained the *Robert E. Lee* and had frequently been victim of Leathers' contemptuous tactics. People compared the two boats, speculating on the speed of their cargo and passenger runs. Newspapers attacked each man's Achilles' heel – pride. The race was inevitable. News that the two vessels would leave New Orleans for St. Louis on June 30, 1870, spread throughout the country, and even as far as Europe.

While people bantered, Captain Cannon said nothing. But shortly before the big day he ordered his men to strip his boat of every excess. Off came the wheel boxing, chains, anchors, windows, doors, spars, cattle dunnage, beds, tables, chairs, chandeliers, heavy curtains and oil paintings. He further rejected freight and passengers. Tom Leathers was unimpressed. He would take Cannon's refused cargo. However, both captains arranged for adequate fuel. They took on pine, resin, candles, tubs of lard, pitch and even discarded bacon fat, and, of course, there were the coal barges that would be stationed along the river.

The morning arrived, crowds gathered, the captains stepped aboard, the gunshot rang out, and at five in the morning the *Robert E. Lee* took off. Nearly five minutes later the *Natchez* slipped away. Thousands of onlookers cheered as she chugged after the *Lee*. At Baton Rouge the *Natchez* was still behind, but Leathers wasn't going to wreck his ship by running it so hard that the boilers would blow up. He would win, alive and with his boat intact. He even stopped to drop off men and freight as scheduled, but with more haste than usual.

The *Lee* was still leading, but the *Natchez* was gaining. Leathers remained confident, and then, north of Natchez the river current surged and the lighter, stripped down *Lee* made great headway. By the time they puffed into Memphis the *Natchez* was an hour behind. On they sped to Cairo, to be hailed by people waving flags and blowing horns. The New Orleans *Picayune* correspondent describes this part of the race: "As we steamed along...the whole country, on both sides of the river seemed alive with a strange excitement, expressed in the waving of handkerchiefs and hats, and running along the shore as if to encourage the panting steamer; and now and then far-off shouts came cheering over the water, and were plainly heard above the roaring of the fires, the clattering of the machinery, the splashing of the water, and the escape of steam."

But Cannon almost met his Waterloo at Cairo. Feeling the exultation of triumph, he stopped to celebrate with drinks for everybody. Suddenly, the craft shook. They were stuck on a sand bar. Minutes passed as the pilot maneuvered. Then with a slow groan the *Lee* was freed. Still, there were consequences to their setback – the *Natchez* had been sighted. With amazing speed old Leathers had gained on them. Now that the two boats were in each other's range, the spirit of rivalry surfaced.

On they pushed, but Cannon kept looking back. He watched the smoke from the chimney of the *Natchez* to gauge the distance between the two boats. Cannon turned his head forward again; he saw something. There was a puff of gray in front of him. It was fog and it was getting thicker. Cannon had to make a decision.

Tom Leathers saw the fog, but there was no dilemma for him.

"Tie'r up!" he shouted. "I'm not crazy."

But John Cannon went on. He felt tense and considered quitting. But in less than an hour the fog lifted. Though past midnight, the night was beautiful again. Behind them, the *Natchez* lay idle at the bank.

The championship was decided. The outcome was no longer debated. At St. Louis on the Fourth of July, people cheered, railroad locomotives tooted, guns boomed and church bells rang. The *Robert E. Lee*, champion of the greatest race that had ever been run on the Mississippi, had made it from New Orleans to St. Louis in 3 days, 18 hours and 14 minutes.

More than six hours later the *Natchez* received an equally rousing reception. That night the captains and townspeople participated in a raucous celebration. But

Leathers insisted that he hadn't lost – his time was certainly better than Cannon's; it was the fog and other delays that caused his defeat. Leathers supporters continue to argue the issue to this day.

Steamboat piloting wasn't confined to the male gender. In the 1880s three women emerged as full-fledged captains. Each woman sought the prestigious position mainly because of money. Their husbands were captains and the frugal wives didn't want to hire a substitute captain when their husbands stayed ashore. Acquiring a license was no mean task. Understandably, men protected their formerly-exclusive profession. "But madam," said the hull inspector, "how can we 'captain' a lady?" He was speaking to the persistent Mary Miller, ·wife of Captain George "Old Natural" Miller, owner of the steamboat *Saline*. On February 18, 1884 she received the coveted gold seal scroll, setting a precedent for future female captains.

Captain Callie French, or "Aunt Callie" as she was known to thousands of patrons of her husband's "New Sensation" showboats, piloted and captained boats from 1888 to 1907. She cooked, mended, nursed, acted, wrote gags, and handled the boat with skill and ease.

The well-loved Captain Mary B. "Ma" Greene first commanded her husband's boat the *H.K. Bedford* in 1897. She took the steamboat from Cincinnati to Louisville during low water and the "lady captain's boat" became extremely popular because of its dependability and air of refinement. Crowds cheered as she piloted the side-wheeler *Greenland* to the St. Louis World's Fair in 1904.

However, long before the appearance of steamboats and their captains, other rivermen wandered to the Mississippi. They led the way in generating the cargo which the boats later carried.

Each summer French fur traders met in Montreal with Indians from the northern lakes for the annual fur fair. Louis XIV of France decreed that occasion as a means of inducing the Indians to deal with the merchants of New France instead of the English at Hudson Bay, Albany or Boston. The Indian trade of the French had never been well-organized, chiefly because of the independent trader, the *coureur de bois*. He hunted without a government license and could do a good business with little capital. He arrived at the Indian village by canoe, exchanged his trinkets for peltries and returned to his market.

Although the illegal procedure of the *coureur de bois* impaired his own countrymen, the Indians were victims of its more lethal impact. Because they were seduced into depending on European trade goods they lost some of their traditions. They were taught to use knives and guns instead of arrows, blankets instead of animal skins and they learned to drink whiskey. They were taught also to strip the river of its fur-bearing creatures rather than to harvest only enough for survival.

Following the defeat of France in the French and Indian War, control of fur trade fell into British hands. To ensure a continuing crop of beaver pelts, the British also encouraged the Indians' taste for whiskey – presuming "the Indians would become excellent hunters in order to satisfy their cravings."

A typical British post was surrounded by a square stockade that incorporated the agent's residence, the men's quarters, a storehouse and a combination workshop, store and clerk's room. Outside the stockade, in a four-acre garden, the British could grow four hundred bushels of potatoes a year. They grew no other vegetable.

Indians supplied the British with a variety of furs: beaver, bear, badger, deer, fox, fisher, lynx, marten, mink, otter, raccoon and muskrat. In turn the British traded an assortment of items: blankets, cloth, gunpowder and shot, tobacco, axes, guns, knives and beaver traps. However, British control of the trade lasted only a few decades along the upper Mississippi because the United States assumed British territory east of the Mississippi after the American Revolution, and west of the river after the Louisiana Purchase in 1803. In time Britain's North West Company relinquished its trade dominance to the American Fur Company.

The American period in fur-trading history had arrived. The American Fur Company, under the auspices of John Jacob Astor, was a big business. Astor, a German immigrant, came to the United States when he was twenty years old. Soon he began to organize the fur trade, buying from Indians in the wilderness and selling to European markets. After the War of 1812 Astor's company became the undisputed king of fur-trading in the Northwest. The American Fur Company had trading posts across the country from Minnesota to Oregon. The company's home base was in New York, but its western headquarters were in Mackinac and St. Louis.

The Minnesota region was divided into two departments – the Northern, or *Fond du Lac*, for trade with the Chippewa (corrupted by Europeans from Ojibwa) and the Western, or Sioux, for trade with the Sioux Indians. Living too far north for an agrarian existence, these two nomadic tribes hunted white-tail deer and buffalo and gathered maple sugar and wild rice for their subsistence. The Ojibwa, who had been forced to migrate west, fought for living space with the Santee Dakota, or Sioux. They executed a decisive victory at their Crow Wing camp in 1768. Now, in 1837, they ceded land to the whites for the first time, making room for settlers. In return for the land, the Indians were given annual payments of money by the United States government. These annuities, as they were called, caused many Indians to neglect or abandon their hunting, for they could now buy goods from the traders with money instead of furs.

After 1837, independent fur traders were active along the east bank of the Mississippi. These traders, like the *coureur de bois*, smuggled in as much liquor as possible to sell to the Indians. This hurt the law-abiding American Fur Company. Naturally, as drunkenness increased among the Indians, hunting declined. But there were other difficulties. The price of furs went down during the great panic of 1837. In European markets the nutria of South America were competing with the nearly extinct beaver. In 1842 the American Fur Company went bankrupt. The fur-trading era was coming to a close and settlement would expand as other extracting industries moved in.

In the 1800s, across a belt from Maine to Minnesota pine fell like dominoes. The "timber cruiser" succeeded the *coureur de bois* and, like his antecedent, he preceded civilization. A cruiser seeks new lumber areas amid the pathless wilderness where thick woods hide the sun and stars. The bold navigator has trained eyes which detect the deflection of tender twigs towards the south. He knows that gray moss is always on the north side of the tree trunk and that the supple and smoother bark is on the east side.

The early cruiser was sometimes accompanied by an Indian who paddled the canoe. In later years he took along a compassman and, on occasion, a cook.

Before the Treaty of 1867 some lumbermen simply entered the Ojibwa land and took the timber. Others paid $1.25 an acre for the government-owned property. After the Treaty the pine land was sold for seven cents an acre. Government surveyors located the land and made it available for purchase. Then the cruisers, representing private lumber companies, arrived and ranged the territory looking for public tracts of land, healthy trees and accessible streams for floating logs in the spring. They needed to accurately estimate acreage and amount of timber in a tract, have excellent retention and, then, disclose the information only to their employers.

In a single decade more than one million pineries passed into the hands of lumbermen and by the 1890s that ownership was limited to a few companies. Frederick Weyerhaeuser founded Minnesota's largest lumber corporation. He emigrated from Germany in 1852 and in 1860 bought a sawmill at the junction of the Mississippi and the Rock River. By 1902 he was president of twenty-one companies. He was the Lumber King.

White pine was the most desirable tree for lumber because it was tall, soft yet strong, odorless and long-lasting. Believing Minnesota's pine forests to be nearly limitless, lumbering companies rushed into the woods to wastefully plunder this priceless natural resource. Towns and farms could be built on the depleted land, the lumbermen reasoned. Much of Minnesota timber went down the Mississippi, in the form of great log rafts, to construct St. Louis, Omaha, Kansas City, Des Moines, Topeka and other cities of the Midwest. It went East and West to be used as building material, and to the West Indies and Brazil as barrels which brought back molasses and coffee. In 1882 the Twin Cities of Minneapolis and Saint Paul used three million feet of lumber and in 1905 Minnesota produced nearly two billion feet. But in the 1920s the great lumber mills, one by one, closed down and Minnesota, which hosted some of the most prolific pine forests in the world, had to get white pine from the Far West.

While lumber companies were for the most part

founded by Yankees from New England, the lumberjacks were of every nationality. French-Canadians, Irish, Germans, Scandinavians, even Indians found work in logging camps. The lumberjacks were "mighty men" who possessed courage and endurance. A typical crew included a foreman, cook, ox-drivers, wood choppers, swampers who cleared roads and slashed the branches from fallen trees, barkers who stripped bark from underneath the logs so they would slide more easily, sled tenders, blacksmiths and the utility man who did a little of everything, including barbering. The lumberjacks labored from dawn to dark throughout the long winter. The trees were felled and cleared of branches, then loaded on sleds and hauled to the river by horses or oxen. There they were rolled onto the ice to wait for the spring thaw.

In the spring lumberjacks guided the logs downriver to the mills, often riding straggling logs. Experts would mount a single log, set it spinning in the water, keep their balance, and, if they wanted to, stop the spin in an instant. Sometimes log jams would occur. Lumbermen risked their lives to clear them. The worst log jam in history happened near Taylors Falls in 1886. The river filled from shore to shore for two miles with 150 million feet of timber. It took the drivers six weeks to get the logs moving again. Logs were branded to identify their owner company or individual; twenty thousand different marks were registered in Minnesota.

Minnesota claims Paul Bunyan, America's best known lumberman. They say Bemidji was his home town. Paul Bunyan was a French-Canadian lumberjack and, though he never stood on American soil, Canadian loggers brought tales of him to their work in the United States forests. The stories were magnified and Paul became a giant – the mightiest man who ever lived. In 1914 the first Bunyan stories appeared in a lumbering trade magazine. Soon newspapers, and even books, were relating the tall tales. All of America knew that Paul had gouged the Mississippi River in northern Minnesota so that his logs could travel to New Orleans and that Babe, Paul's faithful blue ox, formed Minnesota's famed 10,000 lakes with her great hoof prints.

It was through Minnesota's renowned northern lakes that early explorers navigated in quest of the Mississippi's headwater.

Many searched for the source of the Mississippi, and many took credit for its discovery, but Henry R. Schoolcraft found the true head *veritas caput*. He named Lake Itasca from those two Latin names.

Three centuries elapsed between de Soto's unwelcome crossing of the lower Mississippi and Schoolcraft's calculated locating of its beginnings in the Minnesota wilderness. First, Zebulon M. Pike and twenty men ventured north from St. Louis in a seventy-foot keelboat. He was sent by the United States government who had a new interest in the Mississippi Valley, because in 1803, when Louisiana was purchased from France, the entire valley became American territory. When Pike reached Leech Lake he was certain that his mission had been crowned with success, believing he had found the 'main source of the Mississippi'. But Pike was wrong.

The next to search for the headwaters was Lewis Cass, the governor of the territory of Michigan which, at the time, included what is now northeastern Minnesota. In 1820 Governor Cass formed a party of forty, which paddled large freighter canoes and, eventually, arrived at what is today called Cass Lake. Cass was convinced that this was the source of the Father of Waters and headed south feeling satisfied. But Cass Lake was a hundred miles below the target.

Giacomo Costantino Beltrami was the most colorful of the Mississippi explorers. In 1812, when he was 42, Beltrami was exiled from Venice. The wealthy Italian became a gentleman traveler. He absorbed the antiquities of Europe before landing in the United States two years later. There he impetuously decided to take passage on the *Virginia*, the first steamboat to ascend the upper Mississippi.

Throughout the voyage, whenever the captain stopped to gather wood or other supplies, Beltrami went ashore. During one of those stops he wandered into the woods in pursuit of wild turkeys. He became lost and when he found the river, with the help of his compass, the steamboat was nowhere in sight. Beltrami ran along the bank, firing his gun, and eventually, to his relief, he found the *Virginia*. She was aground on a sand bar.

A few months later Beltrami attached himself to Major Stephen H. Long's expedition. Long was commissioned to survey the border between Canada and the United States. On July 7 they started on horseback up the banks of the Minnesota River, a tributary that enters the Mississippi at Minneapolis. In a short time the Italian and the major formed a dislike for each other. Major Long thought Beltrami frivolous and the Italian thought the major stupid. So Beltrami went off on his own.

Following the lead of Pike and Cass, Beltrami decided to look for the Mississippi's headwaters. So he hired an interpreter and two Chippewas to accompany him. On August 14 the little party was ambushed by Sioux, and Beltrami's escorts refused to go on. The Italian soon learned the hazards of canoeing alone; his clothes and gear were soaked from both sides – when the canoe wasn't upset the rains came. The resourceful adventurer rigged his red silk umbrella to cover his soggy equipment.

Eventually Beltrami found a half-breed to guide him to the source, but he took a wrong turn somewhere. They wound up at a heart-shaped lake, instead of the antler-shaped lake that would later be called Itasca. However, it was good enough for Beltrami. Puffed with imagined success he named his discovery Lake Julia. In St. Paul he stepped aboard a steamboat and traveled to New Orleans, still experiencing the glow of victory.

Finally, in 1832, Schoolcraft set out to discover the source. Although he found the true source, his story is dull compared to his predecessors'. Schoolcraft's large assemblage included a military escort. At Cass Lake a smaller detachment of five canoes, each carrying a gentleman passenger and two paddlers, continued with provisions for ten days. They reached Itasca in three days, raised an American flag, fired a volley, named the lake and left in their canoes, this time paddling downstream. Occasional surveyors and missionaries were the only whites to visit Itasca for the next fifty years.

From Itasca, the Mississippi River meanders north and then east before finally taking its proper course south. On the stretch north, the valley sometimes narrows so tamarack and black spruce grow to the rim of the river. In broader spots willow thickets line sedge marshes. Wildlife is abundant along that piece of the Mississippi. Red-winged blackbirds and great blue herons fly over the water; great horned owls sit in the basswood and ash, and deer run through the forests, at times coming to the river's edge.

On the way to Bemidji, where the river turns east, swift currents and sharp bends conceal fallen trees, causing hazardous canoeing. At Crow Wing, halfway from Bemidji to Minneapolis and St. Paul, the wider river flows swiftly and is more easily navigated. Scattered farms surface on the landscape but for miles at a time the river is remote, seemingly untouched by civilization. As a canoeist nears Minneapolis and St. Paul, he is aware of impending civilization. The river is broader and deeper than in most areas on the way down and there are signs of industry. Breweries and flour mills line the banks in spots. Still, views of urban development are relatively sparse, belying the prestige of the two cities. However, even if the buildings are not overbearing, dealing with the locks is. Sitting in a canoe, surrounded by steamboats, must be similar to being in a tugboat which is encircled by ocean liners. The best part of going through the "Twin Cities" is stopping and disembarking for a tour of the towns.

Minnesota's history is linked to water. The waterways made Minnesota a frontier crossroad from America's earliest days. The St. Lawrence from the Atlantic, the Red River via Lake Winnipeg, and the Mississippi from the south have transported voyageurs to Minnesota for centuries. The name Minnesota, chosen by the Sioux, means land of many waters and most likely refers to the 15,000 lakes rather than the numerous rivers.

People have been taking advantage of Minnesota's watery heritage for as long as mankind has been traveling. Ancient mound-builders once roamed the woods and fished the lakes and streams, leaving their massive landmarks for later generations to ponder. More recently, Indians trapped and fished in the dense forests and plentiful lakes, and a band of Norsemen probably explored Minnesota in the 14th century. Other Europeans slowly followed; missionaries and explorers came by way of the rivers in the 16th and 17th centuries. Behind the voyageurs, up the same rivers, came settlers: farmers, trappers, loggers, millers.

The farmers knew that rivers ensured a means of getting their produce to market. Loggers sought Minnesota's forests of white pine, and millers used the power of the rivers to cut logs into lumber or grind wheat into flour. Minnesota was on the way to leading the nation in lumbering and wheat production when the rich iron range was discovered, exposing another aspect of the energetic character of the territory, and of the people who populate it.

Minnesotans live close to nature. Recreational activities abound throughout the state and the natives take advantage of them summer and winter. There's ice-fishing, hockey, skiing, snowmobiling, curling, ice-boating, dog-sledding and snowshoeing in the winter, and sailing, swimming, water-skiing, fishing, wind-surfing, golf and canoeing in the summer. Instead of fighting the cold, Minnesotans celebrate it with some predictable grumbling but fervent participation. Summer's insects cause annoyance but are not a deterrent to camping in the wilderness areas, or to elaborate outdoor soirees in the suburbs of Minneapolis and St. Paul.

Minneapolis and St. Paul, ten miles apart on opposite sides of the Mississippi River, comprise the Twin Cities metropolitan area which contains over two million inhabitants; about half of the state's population. The story of Minneapolis begins in the 17th century when the Sioux and the Chippewa were its sole proprietors. A Franciscan missionary, Father Louis Mennepin, visited the area in 1680 and named the Falls of St. Anthony, which later supplied power for sawmills and the grinding of flour for the first U.S. settlement at Fort Snelling. Pike established the military outpost at the confluence of the Minnesota and Mississippi Rivers and Beltrami met Major Long there, but it was saturated with Scandinavian settlers when Minneapolis was chartered as a city in 1867. Today, the 156 parks and 22 lakes of the city and suburbs commingle with the thriving commerce and culture, creating a physically beautiful cosmopolitan metropolis. In 1959 Irish director Sir Tyrone Guthrie, looking for an alternative to Broadway, established one of the country's finest repertory theaters in Minneapolis.

The Aquatennial, the biggest summer festival in the United States, lasts for one week in July. It incorporates more than 200 sports and entertaining activities, highlighted by an evening "Torch Light" parade. Minneapolis has twice been voted an "All American City" because of its urban renewal program, industrial development, low crime figures, lack of poverty, controlled traffic and care of its less-able citizens.

The influx of Irish-Catholics and Yankees created St. Paul's vastly different character. St. Paul, comparatively conservative, is also culturally advanced. Its beauty is found in its lakes, parks, wide tree-lined boulevards and architecture, of which the State Capitol and Cathedral are two handsome examples.

St. Paul's answer to the Aquatennial, the Winter Carnival, takes place at the end of January and the beginning of February. It includes national ski-jumping championships, cross-country ski races, ice-fishing contests and tobogganing down a slide in front of the State Capitol. Spectators catch a glimpse of the Snowmobile International 500 – a race along a course between Winnipeg, Manitoba and St. Paul.

The Twin Cities have both a cooperative and competitive spirit. They cross over bridges to attend cultural and social events in the other town; they share sports teams, the University of Minnesota, which sits on both sides of the river, and Hubert Humphrey, Eugene McCarthy, Chief Justice Warren Burger and other politicians who have graduated to the national scene.

Though there are several lakes within each city, the lakes are situated in the suburbs. Lumber barons, among other affluent families, built their homes around White Bear Lake, northeast of St. Paul, and those who made their fortune in flour settled on the shores of Lake Minnetonka, west of Minneapolis.

However, though St. Paul has famous stockyards, the Minnesota Mining and Manufacturing Company (3M), and family names like Hill, Ordway, O'Shaughnessy and Weyerhauser, it is esteemed for its preservation of the past rather than its progressive industry. The Union Depot, the St. Paul Hotel and Federal Courts Building are three of the numerous buildings which have been renovated to better display their unique architecture.

The Twin Cities are largely in existence because of the Mississippi. St. Paul, the leading commercial center of the Northwest by the 1860s, grew up because it was the northern limit to steam navigation on the river. Upriver, St. Anthony Falls, the most abrupt drop in the Mississippi from its beginnings at Lake Itasca to its mouth at the Gulf of Mexico, was responsible for the birth of Minneapolis. Led by the power of St. Anthony Falls, Minneapolis became the flour milling center of the world from 1880 to 1930. Pillsbury, General Mills and Cargill, Inc. family heirs still live in the Minneapolis area.

Winona, Prairie du Chien, Memphis and New Orleans are all revitalizing their riverfronts, but Minneapolis has the most ambitious and extensive project. Stretching along fifteen miles of the Mississippi, a river park will capitalize on waterfalls, islands, woods and bluffs and include footpaths and trails for snowshoeing, cross-country skiing and hiking, open spots in the woods for picnicking, and access points for canoeing and fishing in the river.

St. Paul expects to create a wildlife park to protect the hundreds of great blue herons and egrets and the thousands of black-crowned night herons that inhabit a peninsula on the Mississippi. That peninsula, near downtown St. Paul, houses the notorious Pig's Eye sewage plant. A French fur trader and bootlegger named Pierre (Pig's Eye) Parrant, built the first shack within the boundaries of St. Paul in 1838, after being expelled from the Fort Snelling military reservation.

Minnesota claims nearly a third of the Mississippi's entire length. At Minneapolis the river flows through a gorge. From water level much of the city is hidden behind tree-lined bluffs and below the bluffs are small beaches. A few miles downstream, at St. Paul, the riverfront is lined with industrial buildings and barge terminals. Below the Twin Cities the current moves rapidly until it reaches Lake Pepin, a twenty-mile-long widening of the river. The bluffs are four hundred feet high on the Wisconsin side. Fishermen, waterskiers and sailors are scattered on Pepin, but the lake can be a source of anxiety for canoeists and other boaters, because Lake Pepin is also famous for its storms.

Lake Pepin is three miles across at its widest point, and up to 35 feet deep, so a severely cold winter causes thick ice. One spring an unprecedently early rain and thaw caused the river to rise and left a wide space of open water beside the banks on both sides. A southerly wind moved the 25-mile-long, three-and-a-half-feet-thick mass of ice upstream, just above Wabasha. Then the wind blew downstream. Where the river narrowed, the

ice pushed the river bed and railroad track inland. Over 20 feet of ice rested on top of the railroad tracks.

At that point in the river, eagles gather for their spring watch. The fish are forced to swim to the opening at Lake Pepin's mouth, where the eager birds snatch their powerless prey. Captain A. Carr Griffith, a Minnesota steamboat captain, once saw 37 eagles "ice-fishing" near Camp Lacupolis, just above Wabasha.

The commercial intake of fish on the upper Mississippi has remained stable, but the variety of species has declined. The entire river contains more ancient species than any other body of water in the Unites States. Thirty-four Mississippi River fish are included on state lists of endangered species including the paddlefish, alligator gar, sturgeon and alligator snapping turtle. The paddlefish first appeared during the Paleozoic period and today is found only in the Mississippi. They can measure up to six feet in length and weigh more than a hundred pounds, rivaling the other monsters of the Mississippi – the blue catfish and the alligator gar. The sole known relative of the paddlefish lives in the Yangtze River in China. Few continental masses other than the eastern United States and East Asia have retained such large, freshwater drainage systems for so many millions of years. The ancient and extremely deep pools of the Mississippi are rare.

Another ancient remnant appears along the Mississippi. Twenty-five centuries ago, at the end of the Archaic period, Indians built low-relief earthen mounds, apparently for burial purposes. Eventually the mounds were constructed to represent bears, birds, panthers and other animals. Thousands once existed. Though most have been destroyed by erosion and plow, many remain today in St. Paul, southern Wisconsin and northeastern Iowa, among other places. The Effigy Mounds National Monument is located in Iowa across the river from Prairie du Chien. The mounds are the only remnant of a culture that lasted until the twelfth century.

Later, in the seventeenth century, Prairie du Chien (Prairie of the Dog), in Wisconsin, became the major fur-trading post north of the St. Louis. A couple of centuries passed before wise traders, forseeing the demise of the fur trade, turned to lumber and lead.

Lead miners were among the earliest settlers in Wisconsin, Iowa and Illinois. No permanent buildings could be erected by the miners because they knew the Indians would burn them. So they slept in 'badger huts'; holes dug in the hillside. The huts, about the size of a coffin, resembled badger burrows from a distance. Since the miners were Wisconsin's first settlers, the state became known as the "Badger State." The miners came from Kentucky and Tennessee as did the next wave of homesteaders – woodland farmers. They were followed by land-starved Europeans who stayed in the 'Middle Border' states because of the fertile soil.

The history of many states begins with the land, but Iowa has especially productive earth. Nikita Khrushchev even investigated it when he visited the United States. It was the black soil that brought the people into the territory and distributed them evenly across the broad valley that is Iowa. Today, over ninety-five percent of Iowa's land is under cultivation and of the thirty-six million acres, twenty-six million are rated grade A; one quarter of the nation's premium land. Ruth Suckow, one of Iowa's finest novelists, describes her native state: "It combines the quality of a half dozen states; and perhaps that is the reason why it so often seems, and more to its own people than to others, the most undistinguished place in the world...All these diffusing elements, however, are smoothed down with a touch of gentleness into that lovely, open pastoral quality which is peculiarly Iowan after all...Iowa is proud – fairly proud – of its land and corn and hogs. But...has never had the rampant boisterism of Kansas and Minnesota."

Though lead and land attracted frontiersmen, lumber, more than anything else, was responsible for the growth of the upper Mississippi's river towns. Most towns had at least one sawmill. Lumber floated down to market in rafts. A crew of twenty or more steered the thirty-foot-long raft, while a pilot shouted orders. In the center were huts for the oarsmen, the cook and his helper. The largest log raft ever to go down the Mississippi was 270 feet wide by 1,500 feet long. By 1853 sixteen to eighteen rafts were traveling south from spots like Winona in southern Minnesota; La Crosse in Wisconsin; Dubuque, Davenport, Muscatine, Burlington in Iowa; Quincy in Illinois; and Hannibal in Missouri.

At Winona, massive, breathtaking limestone bluffs tower hundreds of feet above the Mississippi; one of them, Sugar Loaf, was a landmark for river pilots. However the hardwood country was finally exploited and logging and sawmills gave way to grain. By 1868 Winona had become the fourth largest wheat market in the country.

Farther downriver, where the Wisconsin bluffs and the river view are magnificent, lies La Crosse, the former lumber town. Today La Crosse is a major grain market as well as a manufacturer of shoes, auto parts and agricultural machinery.

Dubuque, on the Mississippi River opposite the junction of the Wisconsin and Illinois State boundary lines, is the oldest town in Iowa. Dubuque has become the winter quarters for several ships on the upper Mississippi. Close to the river's edge, the business district borders the high bluffs, and back on the hilly plateau is a residential section.

Julien Dubuque settled in the area in 1788. The Fox Indians refused to grant several of his requests, so Dubuque asked his associates to empty a barrel of oil into the Mississippi. While conferring with the Indians around a bonfire, Dubuque grabbed a firebrand and threw it into the water. The sudden burst of flame terrified the Indians. Then, supposedly at Dubuque's command, the fire went out. The Indians conceded all Dubuque asked.

Downstream from Dubuque, below the ironworks and machine shops of Clinton, lie the Quad Cities: Davenport and Bettendorf in Iowa and Rock Island and Moline in Illinois. The four cities stretch along the Mississippi for twelve miles. The first train crossed the Mississippi at Davenport in 1856. That bridge connected with Black Hawk's home, Road Island, Illinois. In the neighboring city of Moline, John Deere established a shop about 1847. There tractors, plows and other farm machinery are still produced.

Because the river turns west on the way to Muscatine, Iowa, a fabulous view of the setting sun is frequent. The town of Muscatine slopes gently down to the river. The buildings are of oxblood brick, and the streets terra-cotta. The nineteenth-century river town has remained in remarkably good working order. The still functioning

J&K Pearl Company is a reminder of the city's title, 'Button Capital of the World.' Someone in Muscatine discovered, in the days before plastics, that the local mussel shells made beautiful buttons.

Below Burlington the Mississippi is divided in two. The channel held to the Iowa side is protected from the turmoil of the rest of the river by an eleven-mile-long wooded island, which eventually fades into a series of sand bars. The channel swings westward and the less-than-a-mile-wide river becomes a mile and a half wide. Canoeing from that point to Nauvoo, Illinois, could be rough going. In 1839, Joseph Smith left Missouri with his Mormon followers and led them to the spot which he named 'Nauvoo'; Hebrew for 'the most beautiful'.

Then the river rushes to Hannibal, where the old Mark Twain Hotel on the waterfront is only the first reminder that 'Samuel Clemens once lived here'. His statue overlooks the river and a statue of two of his characters, Tom Sawyer and Huckleberry Finn, stands near a fence. Hannibal youngsters continue to give the fence a fresh coat of whitewash each year.

The Mississippi turns east near Portage Des Sioux and then suddenly swings south just above the Missouri River. For ten miles the two rivers run together. The next stop is St. Louis and signs of the nearby big city are everywhere: wharves, cranes, barge terminals and commercial docks. A traffic jam of boats could easily dwarf a canoe and, to make matters worse, the river often acts up here. The water gets thick, dark and often shoals into waves three to four feet high. The powerful water could roll logs as big as trees. A canoeist couldn't help but feel fearful to be rocking about in high waves, battling steel barges and the lock's brick wall. Only a glimpse of Eero Saarinen's Gateway Arch alleviates the moment's panic. The arch, 630 feet across its base, was built as a reminder of St. Louis' historic position as gateway to the West. The world's tallest monument is an equalizer because its shadow on the river dominates even the most imposing boat.

However, St. Louis' beginnings were small. And like La Crosse, Prairie du Chien, Ste. Geneviève and New Orleans, its origins were Gallic. In 1764, fourteen-year-old René August Chouteau and a party of men cleared the land at the confluence of the Mississippi and Missouri rivers. They built a trading post at the present-day St. Louis. It became the crossroads of river commerce and westward expansion. Business boomed and, in one decade alone, the population grew from seventeen thousand to seventy-seven thousand.

In a century and a half St. Louis was a great port of call for steamers, and then it became a great railroad and manufacturing center producing everything from shoes to beer. In the 1860s James Eads made engineering history by building his graceful, triple-span, steel arch bridge across the Mississippi at St. Louis. The 'experts' had said that it couldn't be done, but the bridge stands on the same spot today.

St. Louis hosted the first World Fair to have electricity – the Louisiana Purchase Exposition in 1904. The Fair introduced the automobile, ice cream cone and hot dog to an eagerly-waiting world. St. Louis is the home of the famous Clydesdale horses, who reside in a stained glass-windowed stable next door to Anheuser-Busch's Victorian Gothic brewery.

The idea of reviving the waterfront of St. Louis began in 1890 and culminated in the Jefferson National Expansion Memorial. $30 million (twice the price Jefferson paid for the whole territory) was spent to restore some of the romance and history to the original site of St. Louis, where the Gateway Arch now stands.

Raymond R. Tucker, elected in 1953, was Mayor of St. Louis for 12 years. Under Tucker, forty blocks around Archway have been renovated and structures in the immediate area have been restored to preserve the past. Several moored steamboats house restaurants and theaters. The entire Archway section, however, represents only a fifth of the city's total rehabilitation project.

Downriver, at the southernmost tip of Illinois, is Cairo. There Illinois, Missouri and Kentucky meet and the coffee-brown Mississippi contrasts with the steel-blue Ohio. Cairo, whose Egyptian-spelled name is pronounced 'karo,' is farther south than Tunis, Tunisia. An oddity in Illinois, Cairo boasts of gingko and magnolia trees, canebrakes and cottonfields; very much a Southern city.

On the descent to Memphis is New Madrid, Missouri. Wide streets were laid out here in the very beginning, and churches of every denomination placed on them. Worshippers flocked to this so-called 'City of Hope' before the town was forced to move, a victim of earthquakes and floods. The original New Madrid is now under water near the Kentucky shore of the Mississippi. A recent resident recalls, "All the buildings were kept on rollers during my girlhood. Their owners kept rolling them back."

Tennessee, south of Missouri and east of the Mississippi, is famous for sponsoring National Field Trials for Bird Dogs, and claims Davy Crockett, Casey Jones and a wealthy man named John Davis Howard. Howard bought a farm and soon took a leading part in the community affairs of Denver. At local fairs he demonstrated his skill with a revolver. Suddenly he disappeared and it wasn't until Jesse James was killed that the people of Denver realized where he went. He became famous as the hired killer who is credited with gunning down the notorious outlaw.

Tennesseans don't identify their home state by its name alone. They live in West Tennessee, Middle Tennessee or East Tennessee. Reelfoot Lake, in the northeastern part of the state, had a rocky history. In 1908 a group of businessmen formed the West Tennessee Land Company and claimed they owned legal right to Reelfoot. They planned to drain the lake for farmland. The fishermen who derived their livelihood from the resources in Reelfoot took the issue to court and lost. They were unrestrained in their retaliation. A group of angry nightriders abducted two of the land company's officials. One was shot and the other escaped to the bayou. He swam underwater to a log, where he hid while shots were fired into the water for fifteen minutes. The events made front-page news across the country. A few of the nightriders escaped by crossing the Mississippi on a steamboat, but the rest were convicted of murder, though later freed.

As a result of that violence water remains in Reelfoot Lake, and Reelfoot National Wildlife Refuge, comprising 9,586 arces, was established in 1941.

Pleasure boating on the river below St. Louis is minimal, except around Memphis. Memphis sits regally, up on a bluff, in southern Tennessee. Below, canoes glide through the water avoiding waterskiers and motorboaters while picnickers relax on the thousands of sand bars between Memphis and Helena, Arkansas.

Memphis, a city more Midwestern than Southern in character, was established in 1819 by Andrew Jackson and two partners. Jackson named the city after old Memphis, on the Nile in Egypt. It is the largest cotton and hardwood lumber market in the world; it claims the first self-service grocery and drive-in restaurant in the country. It is regarded as a safe and quiet city with the largest medical center in the South; and has won four awards as the nation's cleanest city.

The Cotton Carnival each May rivals the Mardi Gras in New Orleans. A colorful river pageant features the King and Queen of Cotton arriving by boat at the Memphis dock.

Farther downstream, in rich cotton, soybean and rice country is Helena, Arkansas, the state's port city on the Mississippi. In 1834, Mark Twain called Arkansas 'prosperous' stating, "Her gross receipts of money, annually, from all sources, are placed by the New Orleans *Times-Democrat* at four million dollars." Twain continues "Helena occupies one of the prettiest situations on the Mississippi. Her perch is the last, the southernmost group of hills which one sees on that side of the river."

Across the river, with an even higher perspective, the state of Mississippi rises above the watercourse.

In 1699, American-born Pierre le Moyne sieur d'Iberville, an experienced sailor and military commander, planted his colony on the Gulf coast and began to push slowly up the winding rivers. The territory, now the State of Mississippi, was then the center of an Indian population conservatively estimated at 25,000 to 30,000. Of these the three largest groups were the Chickasaw, Natchez and Choctaw tribes. The Chickasaw, whose territory extended northeastward into Tennessee and Kentucky, preferred war to farming. The Natchez lived on the lower Mississippi River, and the Choctaw, largest of all Mississippi tribes, occupied the southern half of the state and a portion of Alabama. The Choctaw disliked war but relished oratory, and specialized in horticulture and diplomacy. Like the meek, they were slowly inheriting the earth; their neighbors could not compete with them economically.

Three tribes lived between the Chickasaw and Choctaw, two traditional enemies, and numerous other trides were scattered throughout Mississippi. They were broad-headed people of a light mahogany complexion and with black hair and eyes. The men, with perhaps the Choctaw excepted, were remarkable examples of physical perfection. According to historians, 'They were tall, well developed, active, with classic features and intellectual expressions; they were brave, haughty, deliberate, and always self-possessed'. The Natchez men stood six feet or more but the average height of the Choctaw was only five feet six inches. Undoubtedly the Choctaw custom of flattening their heads by securing bags of sand to the soft skulls of infant male children, contributed to their small stature. Regardless of their size, the men ruled and the hard-working women were subordinate.

The Indians who moved from the Gulf coast inland, hunted in the winter and farmed and fished in the summer. Rabbits and other small game animals, fish, roots and berries served for food until the corn was ripe. Summer was a season of socializing and making baskets, textiles, wooden and horn objects, pipes and other articles for personal use and trade. The Natchez built fort-like villages with the huts facing a central square. The Chickasaw built a series of long, one-street towns. The Choctaw's settlements resembled extensive plantations with cabins in close proximity to each other.

Indian cabins were made of rough-hewn posts chinked with mud, bark, and, in the lowlands, Spanish moss. The roofs were of cypress or pine bark, or of intermingled grass and reeds. These roofs, skillfully made, lasted 20 years without leaking. A hole was left in the roof to let out smoke from fires which were built in the center of the cabins. However, there were no windows and only one door, an opening about three or four feet high and two feet wide. Inside, the cabin walls were lined with cane beds which were covered with bison skins and used during the day as table and chairs.

The Indians used a stone, a crude hoe made of a large shell or the shoulder blade of a bison, and a stick to make holes for planting. Beans, pumpkins, melons, and sometimes sunflowers were planted with corn, the staple crop. Tobacco was raised as a luxury for men. 'Tom-ful-la' or 'big hominy' and 'bota kapusi' or 'cold corn meal' were favorite dishes. They ate venison, bear, turkey, alligator, crawfish, shellfish, herring, sturgeon and ripe fruits. They drank a mixture of honey and water and acquired a taste for French brandy. There were no fixed times for meals. The tribe gathered together only on the occasion of a feast, when everyone ate out of a bowl which was set in the center. Men sat apart from the women and children.

Clothing was made principally of deer and porcupine skins which were dyed solid colors, embroidered, and made into a breechcloth for the men and a short skirt for the women. Cloaks were made of bird feathers woven into patterns. The women had long, black, shiny hair but men's styles differed within the tribes. The Natchez, for instance, shaved their heads, friar-like, leaving a long, twisted tuft of hair to dangle from the crown down over their left shoulder. To this small feathers were attached. From earliest times the Choctaw and Chickasaw made annual raids west of the Mississippi and brought back bars of silver and copper to be made into ornaments which were worn in profusion. Paint was a necessity and headbands were woven of bison or opposum skin and decorated with beads.

The Indian woman went into the woods alone to give birth, then she returned with her child and resumed her work. The infant was bathed in a nearby stream and, after the age of three, the Natchez and Chickasaw children bathed in the stream daily, summer and winter. Male children were taught to hunt and to fight; female children to prepare food, make the clothing, weave the baskets, mold the pottery and tend the fields. When the boys reached the age of twelve they were committed to the charge of the oldest men, or the Ancients, of their respective families. Under the Ancient's tuition they learned the moral precepts which would regulate their lives. They also learned to run, jump, wrestle, and practice with a bow. The two most skillful marksmen were honored as the 'Young Warrior' and the 'Apprentice Warrior.'

Marriages were never contracted without the consent of the older members of the family, nor were the young people forced into alliances against their will. The Chickasaw warrior painted his face and went to the house of the bride's parents, where she met him at the door. Inside, parents and relatives watched as the young man presented her with a piece of venison, and she gave him an ear of corn. The Natchez couple met at the house of the groom and stood before the oldest man who told them of the duties they were about to assume. Then they exchanged vows similar to those in a Christian marriage ceremony.

A Choctaw warrior approached the girl's maternal uncle, and they agreed on the price, which was also paid to the uncle. Then, on an appointed day, the groom appeared at a designated place to wait until noon. At that time the bride left her parents' lodge and, eluding her gathered friends, ran into the adjacent woods. The female friends of the groom chased her and, if she were anxious for the match, brought her back to the groom's friends. She sat in the middle of a crowd who threw small gifts into her lap. Later she was conducted to a hut adjoining that of her parents. There the groom found her and at sunrise they were called man and wife.

A majority of the tribes believed in a Supreme Being or Great Spirit of the Universe but they had no particular notion of his character, and with the exception of the Natchez, no set form of worship. The Natchez worshipped the sun, which they believed was a male spirit who had molded the first men. All of the tribes maintained superstitions and revered the medicine man and the rainmaker. The medicine man interpreted dreams, charmed away spells and healed the sick; the rainmaker's undertaking was obviously precarious, so he demanded pay in advance. He wasn't contracted until the situation became desperate and, when he failed, he feigned anger. He didn't talk, and secluded himself until it appeared that the weather would cooperate. He told the Indians that if they doubled his fee, the rain would come. The Indians acquiesced and soon the promised rain appeared.

The Natchez were defeated by the French in 1730, causing them to scatter and ending their existence as a tribe. From 1776, when the English rule was challenged by the North American Colonies, the history of the Chickasaw and Choctaw tribes is one of steadily giving way before advancing white settlement and gradually-increasing friction. The Chickasaw and Choctaw ceded all of their possessions in Mississippi and east of the Mississippi River to the United States and moved to Oklahoma, where they established well-defined and stable governments. And so the territory was left for the white man to develop.

The highest point of the Mississippi River rises only to eight hundred feet, and the lowest lands lie at sea level, where the grassy coastal marshes merge with the Mississippi Sound. "To the west, along the Big River," wrote William Faulkner of his native state, once lay "the alluvial swamps threaded by black almost motionless bayous...impenetrable with cane and buckvine and cypress and ash and oak and gum." In the east are the highlands, red clay hills peopled first by the Chickasaws and Choctaws, who were displaced by the proud, taciturn Scotch-Irish. And in the south "the pine barrens and moss-hung liveoaks" surrender to low, treeless marshes which seem "less of earth than water" where they meet the sea.

Onto that coastal plain stepped d'Iberville and his French settlers in 1699 building their log palisade fort at Biloxi Bay. Like later Mississipians, these first Europeans learned that the southern region would never prosper from its soil, and they moved on first to Mobile Bay, then to New Orleans. North of the coastal plain the terrain becomes rolling and the pine trees grow taller. In those thick woods, the topsoil is thin and infertile, also unsuitable for cotton crops. But from the middle of the state to the northeast planters and slaves carved plantations from the rich bottom lands along the rivers and creeks while numerous small farmers struggled to cultivate the red soil of the hillsides.

The Yazoo-Mississippi Delta is a part of the Mississippi River valley flood plain. Because of flood problems, the delta wasn't extensively settled until after the Civil War. As levees were built to hold back the water, the region developed into a plantation society, not of the Old South, but of the New.

The people along the river were independent, forthright frontiersmen who took pride in their Western life style. To the Easterner they had a foreign strangeness – a different dialect and a more abrupt manner. But no one could deny the river's role in boosting the country's economy, or the steamboat's importance in carrying commodities from city to city. The volume of traffic constantly swelled and, in 1846, the number of steamboat arrivals at St. Louis was 2,412, representing 467,824 tons of goods carried.

The boom of the Mississippi intensified the sense of dominion felt by the inhabitants of river towns. The

North and the South might disagree about the abuse of the Indian and the enslavement of the black man, but nothing altered the fact that 'fourteen powerful states and nearly half of the entire population of the United States were coursed by the great river.' Delegates from those states wanted money from Congress for river improvement but their request was denied. Powerful men from the East looked upon the river trade with envious eyes. They endeavored to capture that trade and Henry Clay suggested that a railroad which would connect the southern seaboard with the Mississippi valley and, eventually, the Pacific coast would be invaluable.

The river was especially significant to the cotton-and-slavery system of the South. Many of the cities above St. Louis were sympathetic to the Yankees; those powerful men from the East who pushed for the extension of railroads to the West.

Chicago's lines were the first to link with the eastern railway system. Though the lines touched the Mississippi in seven places the produce was directed East instead of South. Consequently New Orleans dropped from third place as a port city to seventh.

A large portion of travel and trade moved east and west instead of north and south and, to make matters worse for the river people, bridges carrying trains were built over the Mississippi. The first went from Rock Island, Illinois to Davenport, Iowa. However, the thousands of men who made their living on the river were not to surrender without a struggle. Having lost in the case of the 'United States v. Railroad Bridge Company,' they accused the railroad company of deliberately destroying the navigability of the Mississippi by placing the pier in such a way that treacherous currents eddied around it.

As if to prove the point, the steamboat *Effie Afton* got caught in one of the whirlpools that swirled around the long pier. The vessel crashed into the pier four times. Reputedly, at least five men drowned. Suddenly the *Afton* was on fire and spectators on the *Carson*, on shore, and on other boats watched the flames reach the wooden bridge. When the burning bridge fell on the steamboat, whistles blew, dinner bells rang and shouts of victory echoed up and down the river.

However, the railroad builders, no more intimidated than the river men, accused the captain of purposely staging the disastrous scene. The attorney, Abraham Lincoln, intervened requesting 'reason, moderation and compromise.' When the jury returned a verdict in favor of the railroads, the battle was won. However, 'the War' had just begun.

The jungly swamp of willows, cypresses, cane and kudzu vines of the Louisiana shore contrasts with the high bluffs of Vicksburg, Mississippi, across the river. A Confederate cannon, placed partway up the hill on the way to Vicksburg, is only a foreshadowing of the townspeople's allegiance to their ancestors who defended the city.

Vicksburg was a stronghold of the Confederate army. The Union troops took New Orleans and Natchez with ease, but Vicksburg was a different matter.

Thirty thousand Union soldiers moved upriver and quietly landed on the Louisiana side at night. Hearing a strange noise, a slave girl ran out of her house and saw the troopboats on the river. She told a Confederate guard, who wired across the river. Immediately, a centurion mounted his horse and splashed through the rain, heading for Dr. and Emma Balfour's home. The huge, elegant house sat high on a land knob, the focal point of town. The aristocratic Balfours were having a Confederate Ball. The entire downstairs was transformed into lavish ballrooms and anyone who was anyone was there.

The centurion knocked on the door and when Dr. Balfour opened it, he shouted, "The Yankees are coming!" General Remberton stood tall, held his sword high and announced, "Gentlemen, this ball is at an end." The battle began; the Confederates won the first skirmish, but then General Ulysses S. Grant arrived on the scene. He surrounded the entire city, starving out the citizens and military. For forty-seven days, General Grant's soldiers poured shot into the city, using cannons invented by a Frenchman. The townspeople dug caves to avoid the bombardment of cannonballs which traveled four miles. Mr.s. Balfour bought a cave for five hundred dollars. But it was 'horrible-claustrophobic', so she went home to 'take her chances'. Her house was hit, but Emma Balfour continued to place food on a porch table for passing Confederate soldiers, and to feed the officers corn bread and milk.

The forty-seven-day siege ended July 4th, 1863, and Independence Day wasn't celebrated in Vicksburg until President Dwight Eisenhower came for a visit a hundred years later.

Emma Balfour died in 1900, long before that reconciliation. Two blocks down from the Balfour house, high on the same hill, is the Courthouse, converted by Southerners into a hospital for wounded Union men. That Courthouse, untouched during the war, is still standing. The Balfour house, Union headquarters after the siege, also stands today.

In its surging passage below Vicksburg, the Mississippi comes to a high hill – two hundred feet of red-brown bluff, crowned by vines of wild grapes amd masses of oak. The river seems to change there. It makes a wide semicircle, then the silver waterway, sun-splashed with yellow, continues to slide towards the Gulf of Mexico.

Overlooking the Mississippi from a series of lofty palisades is Natchez, one of the earliest white settlements in the state of Mississippi and a one-time center of antebellum culture. From the ancient plaza, dating from the days of the Spaniards, streets, lined with aged trees, fan out in every direction.

Though the Second World War reduced ties to former times, reminders of the romantic Old South still linger in Natchez. A pilgrimage in March or April recalls the plantation days when men in morning coats, and lovely girls carrying parasols, strolled the grounds of magnificent French and Spanish-influenced homes and flawlessly-manicured gardens.

'Longwood', one of the more eccentric manor houses, is regionally referred to as Nutt's Folly. Ornate galleries surrounding the six-story octagonal house were crowned with an onion-shaped dome and thin steeple. Inside, the thirty-two, eight-sided rooms were filled with statuary from Italy and Greece. Next, an artificial lake was dug near gardens which produced growth from imported plants, but early one morning, in 1861, a horseman raced up to Longwood. War had started and Dr. Haller Nutt's 'Folly' was never completed.

Centuries ago buffalo beat a path between Nashville, Tennessee, and Natchez, Mississippi. They returned year after year to their historic feeding grounds and salt licks. The huge beasts were followed by the Choctaw and Chickasaw, frontiersmen, highwaymen, armies, the U.S. mails and modern surveyors. The flatboatmen who drifted downstream on boats which were torn apart, used the path to return North. The murder victims of John Murrell and other outlaws were found on the Natchez Trace; Andrew Jackson and his Tennesseans followed the same trail on the way to meet the British in New Orleans; Aaron Burr was arrested for treason below gigantic oak trees beside the path; and Meriwether Lewis met death by treachery as he traveled over the passage. The stories continue, as the Trace reaches to Louisiana.

On the banks of the Mississippi River, about a fourth of the way down into Louisiana, the Indians had stripped a cypress tree of its bark and painted it red to mark the boundary between the Houma and Bayogoula hunting grounds. When Sieur d'Iberville and his men found the post they called it *baton rouge* or red stick. Baton Rouge is the capital of Louisiana. More national flags have flown over Baton Rouge than any other state capital: French, Spanish, British, West Florida, Louisiana Republic, Confederate and United States. Their Pentagon Building, the forerunner of the Pentagon in Washington, once housed Braxton Bragg, Philip Sheridan, Stonewall Jackson, Robert E. Lee, Jefferson Davis, Wade Hampton, and John A. Le Jeune.

Traveling on a steamboat in the 1800s, within 200 miles of New Orleans, a man could see magnificent plantation houses on both sides of the river and along the bayous. The tall, pillared, white residences were built by wealthy cotton and sugar cane growers. Cultivated fields of tassel-topped sugar and long, low rows of grayish-white cotton balls came down to the levee's edge, and all around was the lush foliage of the semi-tropics; clumps of live oak and cypress hung with Spanish moss, huge flowering bushes of camellias and magnolias, hedges of roses and the sharp-pointed palmettos and Spanish dagger.

Sugar cane had first been planted in Louisiana in 1700 and cotton in 1718, but it wasn't until the development of sugar refining and the invention of the cotton gin in the last decade of the eighteenth century that the two crops fully realized commercial success. Other factors contributed to the prosperity of the harvests: the mild climate and fertile soil; the preponderance of slave labor, and the Mississippi and its complicated network of waterways which provided economical transportation to New Orleans, where vessels from all over the world were tied up two and three deep along the miles of waterfront.

New Orleans was established as a European city for nearly a century before it became a part of the United States. In spite of forty years of rule by Spain, its culture and language remained entirely French up to the time of the Louisiana Purchase.

The city had an unfavorable beginning. "New Orleans was built in a place God never intended a city to be built...six feet below sea level in the middle of a swamp, squeezed between a giant river and a huge lake..." The French called it *Le Flottant* – The Floating Island and *La Prairie Tremblante* – The Shaking Prairie. The English forebodingly named it the Wet Grave. Water has forever been the city's source of distress and its means of survival. Today, New Orleans, the only major city in the United States that lies below sea level, also has the most rainfall: from 54 to 64 inches a year.

The Mississippi River, primarily responsible for the city's prosperity, has also contributed to some of its many catastrophes. Floods, hurricanes, tornadoes, countless fires and plagues of yellow fever and cholera have assaulted New Orleans. But New Orleans weathered those storms and evolved in three distinct phases.

The original French city, Vieux Carré (Old Square), more frequently called the French Quarter, surrounds Jackson Square, renamed after the War of 1812. St. Louis Cathedral, the oldest active cathedral in the country, stands at one end of the Square. The French Quarter was rebuilt during the period of Spanish rule, after a fire in 1788 had destroyed four-fifths of its buildings. Following the Louisiana Purchase, Americans coming to New Orleans were so completely ostracized by the Creoles that they built their own city on the other side of Canal Street, and for a while New Orleans existed as two separate communities. American society constructed its lavish homes in the Garden District, while Creole families erected their elegant houses up Esplanade Avenue on the other side of the French Quarter. It remained a divided city until the Americans prevailed through force of wealth and sheer numbers. The term

'Dixie' originated when bilingual banknotes were printed with '10 dollars' on one side and the French *dix* on the other, and were nicknamed 'dixies'. Until the popular Civil War song associated the term with the entire South, only New Orleans was called Dixie.

The third New Orleans has been built since World War II, after modern technology found a means of constructing skyscrapers on the city's soggy soil.

Though French, Spanish and Anglo-Saxons composed the largest part of the population of New Orleans, Germans, Italians and Africans were present. The free people of color, the *gens de couleur*, comprised an important element in the city, until the Civil War erased class distinction among the blacks. Young Creole gentlemen customarily took beautiful quadroons as their mistresses, established them in houses, provided for their futures and fathered their children.

To fill the immense empty spaces of its Louisiana Territory, after the supply of criminals and political refugees was exhausted, France devised the Mississippi Company and placed it in the control of an inventive and unscrupulous Scot, John Law. Law depicted an investment in Louisiana as a guarantee of wealth and happiness. Frenchmen (and later, Germans) were tempted by pictures of Indians pouring gold, silver and pearls at the feet of colonists, who offered mere trinkets in exchange.

Many of the deceived souls, who sacrificed everything they owned to invest in the misrepresented land, never lived to see it. And those who survived the ocean voyage discovered that the new land was not a nirvana. Riffraff from French prisons and aristocratic political refugees brought danger as well as color. Crime was rife.

Nevertheless, a section of the swamp was cleared and nearly a century later, when it became part of the United States, the city consisted of one hundred square blocks. Drainage ditches surrounding each block were so often filled with water that for many years blocks were known as 'islets.' The perimeter of the town was palisaded and moated, with forts at each corner – thus the name Rampart Street at the edge of Vieux Carré. The first houses were crudely constructed of cypress slabs chinked with mud and Spanish moss, and roofed with palmetto thatch. Though the majority of dwellings were primitive, wealthy colonists filled them with fine furnishings from France and ornamented themselves with opulent raiment.

In the early stages of the town's development a shipment of young women was sent from France to be wives of the settlers. They were called 'casket' girls (from *filles à la cassette*) because each was provided with a chest of clothing and linens as a dowry. In 1727 a group of Ursuline nuns arrived to look after the young women and to educate their offspring. The Ursuline Convent, constructed in 1734, is said to be the oldest building still standing in the Mississippi valley. The diary of one of the nuns describes the city as she found it, following a perilous crossing:

"Our town is very handsome, well constructed and regularly built...The streets are large and straight. The houses well built, with upright joists, the interstices filled with mortar, and the exterior whitewashed with lime. In the interior they are wainscoted. The roofs of the houses are covered with shingles which are cut in the shape of slates, and one must know this to believe it, for they all have the appearance and beauty of slate...I do not, however, speak of the manners of the laity, but I am told that their manners are corrupt and scandalous. There are, however, a great number of honest people, and one does not see any of those girls who were said to have been deported on compulsion...The women here are extremely ignorant as to the means of securing their salvation, but they are very expert in the art of displaying their beauty. There is so much luxury in this town that there is no distinction as far as dress goes. The magnificence of display is equal to all. Most of them reduce themselves and their families to the hard lot of living at home on nothing but sagamité [hominy cooked with meat or fish], and flaunt abroad in robes of velvet and damask, ornamented with the most costly ribbons. They paint and rouge to hide the ravages of time, and wear on their faces, as embellishment, small black patches."

The overstated display of luxury in such a primitive environment became even more pronounced a few years later when Bienville was succeeded by a new Colonial Governor, Pierre Cavagnal de Rigaud, Marquis de Vaudreuil, in 1743. The Marquis and his wife brought the ostentatious elegance of the court at Versailles to the muddy streets of the frontier settlement. Continual

balls and banquets featured guests adorned in silks, satins, velvets and lace. Fine wines and sumptuous foods were served in crystal and gold-plated china. The colonists loved it.

In recent decades another source of wealth has come to New Orleans. Large numbers of tourists, attracted by the romantic atmosphere of the French Quarter, the peerless cuisine of intimate restaurants and the excitement of Mardi Gras, migrate to the city.

Creole cuisine, developed in the city's early days, continues to be one of its integral characteristics. The fare is rich and highly seasoned, but mild compared to the meals served in the eighteenth and nineteenth centuries. Three factors contribute to the success and longevity of the American cooking tradition: the unique plenty of native ingredients, particularly seafood; the mixture of nationalities that made up the city; and the influence of the French for whom eating is serious business. In 1727 the same Ursuline nun who described the dicotomy of the crude frontier listed the available foods: "...wild beef, venison, swans, geese, fowls, ducks, *sarcelles* [a type of small, wild duck], pheasants, partridges, *cailles* [small birds similar to partridges], and fish: catfish, carp, bass, salmon, besides infinite varieties not known in France." There were "wild peas and beans and rice; pineapples, watermelons, potatoes, *sabotins* [a kind of eggplant], figs, bananas, pecans, pumpkins." They drank "chocolate and *café au lait* every day," and ate "bread made of rice or corn mixed with flour...and sagamité" [an early form of jambalaya].

And then there's shrimp, oysters, crabs, red fish, trout, okra, mirltons prepared in the French manner and flavored with Spanish, Italian, African and American Indian seasonings. New Orleans has long boasted of a Creole dish called gumbo, served in a soup bowl with a teacup-molded mound of rice in the center and surrounded by crab claws in a sauce with native ingredients and international spices.

A mystique envelops New Orleans coffee. Dripped very slowly and often blended with chicory, it is preferred "so strong that a spoon will stand up in it," and it must be "black as the devil and hot as hell." Thus the name, *café brûlot diabolique*, the devil motif on the brûlot cups, and the devil figurines on the base of the brûlot chafing dish. Café brûlot is made from a very strong coffee added to a flaming mixture of brandy, sugar, cinnamon, cloves, and citrus peel.

New Orleans' oldest and most famous restaurant, Antoine's, has remained in the family since being founded in 1840 by Antoine Alciatore, and is housed in the original building with the French Quarter's distinctive, intricately designed ironwork balconies. The restaurant began as a dining room for live-in guests, but young Antoine brought epicurean recipes from France and created many more. The lodgers are long gone and forgotten, but the food remains famous.

Jazz, another mainstay on New Orleans, was born and nurtured in its nightclubs. The music remains authentic in the Maison Bourbon and Preservation Hall. This music, performed mostly by blacks, which began as accompaniment to weddings, funerals, dances and parades became known as 'blues'. St. Louis, Chicago and New York adopted the Southern sound. Later, in 1917, the orchestral style called New Orleans jazz was popularized by the Original Dixieland Jazz Band, preserved on records by the 1923 groups of Joseph 'King' Oliver and 'Jelly Roll' Morton.

However, New Orleans' most spectacular show is the Mardi Gras, a custom imported from France. The extravaganza attracts thousands of visitors each year. The carnival season incorporates several weeks of masked balls, parades, parties and general frivolity, culminating in Shrove Tuesday or Mardi Gras ('Fat Tuesday'), the day before Lent begins.

West of New Orleans, bordering the Gulf of Mexico, is a region crisscrossed by endless stretches of swampland and filled with myriad streams or bayous. It is a place of moss-draped beauty, a maze of water and swamp where turtles and alligators sun on logs, birds of every description flutter among the entangled cypress and live oak, and winding roads follow the meandering bayous past white-columned plantation houses.

This is Cajun country.

In 1717 France ceded Nova Scotia, then Acadia, to Britain. The Acadians remained loyal to France so, in 1755, the British decided to deport them. Several thousands were expelled. Many left before receiving their deportation orders. Some returned to France, others went to the British colonies in Massachusetts and Georgia, but most found their way to southern Louisiana, where a proportion of the population already spoke French. Those hardy aliens plowed land and continued to practice their Catholic religion, while trying to acclimate to the extreme heat.

Longfellow chronicled those hard times in his poem, *Evangeline*. The New England poet never visited Louisiana but preserved for American folklore the legend of the Acadians through the tragic story of Evangeline making the long trek from Nova Scotia to Louisiana in search of her sweetheart. According to legend, Longfellow's poem was inspired by the story of Emmeline Labiche, whose statue now stands in the St. Martinville churchyard, near the old Acadian cottage which belonged to her lover. St. Martinville, on Bayou Teche, experienced a brief period of glamor when fugitives from the French Revolution made it "a pretty little village...full of barons, marquises, counts and countesses," but the mid-nineteenth century yellow fever epidemic, Civil War and diversion of trade from bayou to railroad brought about the city's demise as 'Little Paris'. Still, the Bayou Teche and Bayou LaFourche regions are as lovely as any in Louisiana, and their people have preserved the Acadian customs and their simplicity of life style.

The Cajuns, physically isolated from the rest of America, have clung to their old ways, remaining one of the least assimilated peoples in the United States. Speaking an ancient French dialect which few outsiders, including people from France, understand, mixing little with the modern world, their livelihood comes from the more primitive occupations of fishing, boating, trapping, and selling hand-woven baskets and cloth. Moss gatherers cure the silver-gray Spanish moss on piles of pecky cypress until it becomes a black, resilient, fibrous mass. The cured, springy moss is used to stuff furniture. In this region of few roads they live on wooden houseboats and are transported by pirogues, slender canoes hollowed out of cypress logs.

The pirogue race is just one of their uncommon traditional forms of entertainment. The Cajuns like to celebrate their unique talents. At the Cameron Fur and Wildlife Festival the men set up to twelve traps a minute while the women compete in muskrat and nutria skinning contests. They dance and sing at the 'Crayfish

Festival' but the 'fais-do-do' of the year is the Cajun country Mardi Gras. Bearing little resemblance to its sister gala in New Orleans, the festivities begin when a band of masked and costumed riders, led by the "capitaine", circle the community in search of ingredients for a gigantic gumbo. The gumbo will be prepared in the afternoon to serve two hundred people in the evening, and citizens gladly contribute their fattest chicken and spiciest sausage for the epicurean delight.

The merrymaking is highlighted by an evening dance, and like everything else that is inherently Cajun, their music is reminiscent of nothing else. The *joie de vivre* is epitomized in the attitudes of the accordion, fiddle and triangle players who dance a jig while entertaining with their instruments.

Another source of pleasure for Cajuns and other river folk came in the form of a stern-wheel boat.

The *Polly*, better known as the "candy boat" by residents of river towns, was owned by Anderson Gratz of New York and piloted by Captain Griffith.

Dr. Walter Bullick, from Lexington, Kentucky, rode on the *Polly* and treated river people from Minnesota to Louisiana. Besides medical supplies the boat carried bolts of cloth, baseballs, bats, balloons and 189 pounds of peppermint candy sticks. The perforated candy, wrapped in waxed paper and double-dipped in paraffin, would float for a day or more before being damaged. Thousands of youngsters who lived beside the bayous and tributary rivers excitedly anticipated the "candy boat's" approach.

For the Louisiana bayou people, the *Polly's* presence could only be equalled by a holiday. Moss gatherers, fishermen, trappers and their families swarmed up the narrow streams, pushing their canoes with oars, to meet her.

Much folklore surrounds the alligator, but Captain Griffith recalls a real-life mishap. "We were near Morgan City, Louisiana and I decided to chase a huge bullfrog that looked to weigh five pounds. The water was covered with scum and hyacinth, so all I could see was two eyes, set far apart, when he stuck his head up. I grabbed the frog, but...it was an alligator, and I had him

behind the neck. The only safe way to hold an alligator, if you're strong enough, is to keep his mouth closed with an index finger and thumb. Needless to say, I let go immediately." Another story about alligators probably isn't true-to-life.

The passenger who was going down the Mississippi River for the first time in his life secured permission to climb up beside the pilot, a grim old greyback, who never told a lie in his life.

"Many alligators in the river?" inquired the stranger, after a look around.

"Not so many now, since they got to shootin' 'em for their hides and taller," was the reply.

"Used to be lots, eh?"

"I don't want to tell you about 'em, stranger," replied the pilot, sighing heavily.

"Why?"

"Cause you'd think I was a-lying to you, and that's sumthin' I never do. I kin cheat at cards, drink whiskey or chaw poor terbacker, but I can't lie."

"Then there used to be lots of 'em?" inquired the passenger. "I'm 'most afraid to tell ye, mister, but I've counted 'leven hundred allygaters to the mile from Vicksburg clear down to New Orleans! That was years ago before a shot was ever fired at 'em."

"Well, I don't doubt it," replied the stranger.

"And I've counted 3,459 of 'em on one sand bar!" continued the pilot. "It looks big to tell, but a government surveyor was aboard, and he checked 'em off as I called."

"I haven't the least doubt of it," said the passenger with a sigh.

"I'm glad 'o that, stranger. Some fellows would think I was a liar when I'm telling the solemn truth. This used to be a paradise for alligators, and they were so thick that the wheels of the boat killed an average of forty-nine to a mile!"

"Is that so?"

"True as a Gospel, Mister; I used to almost feel sorry for the cussed brutes, 'cause they'd cry out e'enamost like a human being. We killed lots of 'em, as I said, and we hurt a pile more. I sailed with one captain who allus carried 1,000 bottles of linimen to throw over to the wounded ones!"

"He did?"

"True as you live, he did. I don't 'spect I'll ever see another such Christian man. And the allygaters got to know the "Nancy Jane", and to know Captain Tom, and they'd swim and rub their tails against the boat, and purr like cats, and look up and try to smile!"

"They would?"

"Solemn truth, stranger. And once when grounded on a bar, with an opposition boat right behind, the allygaters gathered around, got under the stern, and humped her clean over the bar by a grand push. It looks like a big story, but I never told a lie yet, and never shall. I wouldn't lie for all the money you could put aboard this boat."

There was a painful pause, and pretty soon the pilot continued:

"Our injines give out once, and a crowd of allygaters took a tow line and hauled us forty-five miles upstream to Vicksburg."

"They did?"

"And when the news got along the river that Captain Tom was dead every allygater in the river daubed his left ear with black mud as a badge of mourning, and lots of 'em pined away and died."

The passenger left the pilot house with the remark that he didn't doubt the statement, but the old man gave the wheel a turn and replied:

"There's one thing I won't do for love nor money, and that's make a liar out of myself. I was brung up by a good mother, and I'm going to stick to the truth if this boat doesn't make a cent."

South of New Orleans, a scraggy peninsula of marsh and leveed land flanks the Mississippi as it stretches into the Gulf of Mexico. Six times in this century hurricanes have spun out of the Gulf to spill the sea across farms and homes, most recently with *Camille*, in 1969.

But citrus growers stay; they patiently plant again because the black soil, the best clay from as far away as Canada, is just right for citrus orchards. The soil, drained from 31 states and two Canadian provinces, reaches Southeastern Louisiana where the world's fourth longest river system marshalls to the sea through many mouths. The Mississippi drops its sand, silt and clay to form the delta across the continental shelf. At least half a dozen times since the end of the last ice age, the river has changed course dramatically, abandoning an earlier delta to erosion and creating the new deltic plain that forms much of the Louisiana coast.

The modern delta – the Balize – was only 300 years old in 1682, when La Salle paddled down the Mississippi. The French, installed in the early 1700s, were followed by Germans, Creoles, Acadians expelled from Canada, Spaniards, Anglo-Americans, Blacks, Yugoslavs, Italians, Irish, Chinese, Filipinos and Vietnamese. Courageous frontiersmen, opportunists, immigrants and refugees merged at the river's mouth. Habitants of river and sea also merge at the mouth. The delta marsh and the esturine areas around it comprise the source of the entire Gulf fisheries and Louisiana's lead in the nation's catch.

However, if not for the U.S. Army Corps of Engineers flood-control formation above Baton Rouge, the Mississippi would be changing course to follow the Atchafalaya on route to the sea, a course 140 miles shorter than its present one. The tributary river already siphons off 25 percent of the Mississippi's water and has a fledgling delta of its own, among the youngest in the world. If nature had its way the Balize Delta, over a period of time, would simply disappear. Cut off from the river's fresh water, and its replenishing flood-borne silt, a forsaken delta sinks in its own weight and is then at the mercy of uncontrolled erosion.

The Corps of Engineers want to corral the Mississippi, but their uphill battle is complicated by man's interference. There are levees south of New Orleans and, northward to Baton Rouge, levees keep nearly two million people dry. Consequently, the delta's marshlands, largely cut off from their life's source, are both starving and dying of thirst. Aerial mapping his revealed the loss of 850 square miles of Louisiana's deltaic plain since 1956.

Levees deny marshes new layers of silt and fresh water; canals hasten erosion, and hurricanes cause damage that does not heal. Scientists fear losing both wildlife habitat and ridge land where Louisianians live. That land is precious because the marsh supplies ample sustenance to the deltans who dwell within its reach. The oysters, catfish, redfish and shrimp often comingle in a gumbo or jambalaya, and waterfowl furnish first-rate hunting on the marsh, a major wintering ground. Thousands of passerine birds arrive in spring; weary from their travels across the Gulf, they descend on the first piece of land in that watery space. Southbound teal come in late summer, followed by scores of other ducks and, finally, the geese trumpet down from the north to feed on ragged grasses bordering the sea.

Many deltans make their living from land, water and sky. They shoot birds and catch catfish in trotlines and traps most of the year. They trap nutria and racoons for fur in the winter, hunt alligators in the fall, and trawl for fish and shrimp in season.

The shrimp catch, principal source of income for small-scale independent Louisiana fishermen, grew from an annual average of 41 million pounds in the 1930s to a record 91 million in 1982. And commercial shrimpers' numbers increased elevenfold to a present 17,000. Beyond that, sportsfishermen are entitled to a daily catch of 100 pounds per boat for private use.

The oil industry has played a part in the pressure on the coast's wildlife resources and the encounter between man and marsh. Today, the typical deltan works in a store or factory or on a crew boat or drilling rig. The oil industry has provided jobs for people at the expense of the environment. More than 22,000 wells have been drilled in the Gulf, with 4,000 intruding. Nine out of ten are off Louisiana, and forests of steel surround the delta.

However, the real fortunes are not made by watermen, but owners and leaseholders of marshland who received bonuses in mineral royalties.

The delta is a metaphor for the whole Mississippi. Though magnified in the delta, all along the river the loss of wetlands is an ecological fact. A resource as great as the Mississippi must be used and therefore, the negative by-products of pollution, erosion, siltation and urbanization do exist. The hope is that those problems are being recognized and reconciled. The new riverfront parks, on the Mississippi's urban and untamed shores, is another reason for optimism and another evidence of change.

The proud, floating palaces gliding up and down the Mississippi with majestic grace, bringing excitement to every stop, the riverboats carrying an assemblage of people who had been places and seen things that those confined to shore could never imagine; the riverboat captains who knew every curve in the river and the card sharks who knew every trick in the deck; the fancy folk who became epicureans along the way and the inquisitive youth who were lured to the river for a spell of fantasy and freedom, will not be forgotten.

(Previous page) the dome of the Old Courthouse amid the
skyscrapers of St. Louis. (These pages) the Mississippi
River and the soaring Gateway Arch, symbol of St. Louis
as the "Gateway to the West" and the central feature of
the Jefferson National Expansion Memorial.

(These pages) the Gateway Arch, designed by Eero
Saarinen, is 630 feet high and required 886 tons of
steel to build. (Left) the riverfront quay provides the
link between modern St. Louis and its historic past, as
riverboats still ply the Mississippi's waters.

St. Louis is the largest city in the State of Missouri, being of great agricultural importance as well as a leading industrial center. Immigrants who came to the city would often travel on riverboats such as shown (opposite page). (Above) the graceful Gateway Arch.

(Above) water lilies in the Missouri Botanical Gardens,
outside the Climatron (opposite page). Enclosed in
rigid plexiglass, this structure is the world's first
geodesic domed greenhouse and houses a wide collection
of subtropical and tropical plants.

Nymphaea
"Mrs. George C.
Hitchcock"

(Above) the stern-wheeler *Robert E. Lee,* now a floating restaurant on the river. (Opposite page) Gateway Arch frames the Old Courthouse, which was once the scene of slave auctions and where the pre-Civil War Dred Scott slavery case was heard.

(This page, above) *The Runner* at Kieer Plaza with the Old Courthouse beyond. (Top right and opposite page) gleaming Gateway Arch dominates the city skyline. (Right) the Greek Revival-style Old Cathedral was built in 1831-34.

(This page, above and far left) Gateway Arch symbolizes St. Louis' role as the gateway of westward expansion. It was from here that Lewis and Clark set out on their historic expedition in 1804, and here also that fur-trading enterprises had their bases. Pioneers who wished to follow the California, Oregon and Santa Fe Trails also came here. (Left, top left and opposite page) the riverboat *Tom Sawyer*, named after the character created by Mark Twain, who also wrote *The Adventures of Huckelberry Finn*.

St. Louis lies on the Mississippi below the confluence with the Missouri River. Pierre Laclède Liguest, of New Orleans, chose the site in 1764 with the intention of making it a fur-trading post. Auguste Chouteau helped establish a village here and named it after King Louis IX of France (1214-1270), who led the Sixth Crusade to the Holy Land in 1248 and was canonized by Pope Boniface VIII in 1297. The settlement was ceded to Spain in 1770, but was later transferred back to French control. By the Louisiana Purchase of 1803 it became part of the United States. Cobblestones bedeck streets in the downtown area (below, right and far right). (Bottom right) Bingham's café. The Old Cathedral (opposite page, right of picture) was built in limestone on the site of the original log church of the 1770s.

South of St. Louis lies Sainte Genevieve. The first permanent white settlement in Missouri, it was established by French Canadians in 1735. However, Philippe Renault of Paris had already come to the region, in 1723, with Guinea Negroes and French laborers to mine for lead. Bolduc House (this page) was built in the early 1780s and has now been restored. It was the home of a wealthy merchant and planter, Louis Bolduc, who had interests in lead mining. Today, it is one of the few remaining Mississippi Valley houses of the 18th century. Old-style architecture graces Sainte Genevieve (opposite page), such as that found on Merchant Street (top left and top center). (Bottom right) on the Old Brick House the legend reads, "First Brick Building West of the Mississippi – 1785"; (bottom left) Antoine Parfait Dufour House, 1790.

The mighty Mississippi is one of the world's busiest
commercial waterways, with many vessels carrying
cargoes. (Above) pusher tug and lighters ply the river,
which acts like a major artery running through the
center of this great industrialized nation.

(This page) scenes in Sainte Genevieve. (Far right) antique shops on Main Street. (Below) Joseph Oberle House of 1874. (Bottom right) St. Gemme Beauvais House of 1848. (Opposite page, top right) goods train carrying freight for river haulage. (Bottom left) boxcar containing lime at a Sainte Genevieve railhead. The city is famous for quarrying and processing lime. The Sainte Genevieve Limestone Formation, laid down over 325,000,000 years ago, was so named because of exposures studied in bluffs along the Mississippi near to the city. (Bottom right) the ferry boat. (Top left) the Mississippi at Cape Girardeau.

MISSOURI
PACIFIC
LINES

11960

Some ten miles north of Cape Girardeau lies the Trail
of Tears State Park, a 3,346-acre tract of land where
high bluffs overlook the Mississippi (above). Through
here the Cherokee marched on their forced journey from
Tennessee to Oklahoma. (Opposite page) Lake Boutin.

FATHER JACQUES MARQUETTE
1673-1975

In 1672 Louis Joliet and Father Jacques Marquette were commissioned by King Louis XIV to discover the course of the Mississippi River. On June 17, 1673, the expedition entered the Mississippi from the Wisconsin River and began its descent by canoe.

On July 4, 1673, the seven-man expedition passed the mouth of the turbulent Missouri River and later observed the confluence of the Ohio and Mississippi. Upon reaching an Arkansas Indian village near present Helena, July 17, they were certain that the Mississippi flowed into the Gulf of Mexico. Fearful of the Spanish if they continued southward, at this point Father Marquette and Joliet turned back.

A dedicated and gentle priest, Father Marquette first brought the word of God into the Mississippi Valley, gave the world an account of its lands and, with Joliet, laid the basis for France's claim to the area.

Born at Laon, France, June 1, 1637, Father Marquette died April 18, 1675, on the eastern shore of Lake Michigan from the hardships of his missionary life.

ERECTED BY THE MISSOURI MARQUETTE TERCENTENARY COMMISSION

(Left) commemorative plaque to the explorer and Jesuit priest, Father Jacques Marquette. (Right) tranquil Lake Boutin. (Below) a pusher tug on the river's bank, capable of driving ahead of it a vast raft of barges. However, it was back in 1917 that the steamer *Sprague* set a new world record for size of tow with her raft of 60 coal barges, which covered an area of 6.5 acres and weighed 67,307 tons! (Bottom right) grain silos at Caruthersville. Laid out in 1857, the city was named after Congressman Samuel Caruthers. A few miles north is the site of La Petite Prairie, a settlement of 1794 which was almost totally destroyed by earthquake in 1811. (Opposite page) a swamp near New Madrid. Floods and changes in the Mississippi's course meant moving the city's site several times.

The elegant stern-wheeler *Memphis Queen III* (these pages) glides along the Mississippi, a reminder of a stately, bygone age when "palaces on paddlewheels" steamed the length of the river.

Riverboats line the banks at Memphis, Tennessee. Andrew Jackson, later President of the United States, helped to found the "Town of Memphis" in 1819. It was named after the ruined capital of ancient Egypt, on the banks of the Nile, because of its situation overlooking another great river; the Mississippi.

Rival riverboats at Memphis; a reminder of the days when captains were wont to race each other down the "Father of Waters". The most famous occasion was the race in 1870 between the *Natchez* and the *Robert E. Lee*, which the latter won, parts of its superstructure having been removed to save weight.

(These pages) downtown Memphis seen from Mud Island. The city itself serves one of America's principal cotton-growing regions, and it is to this crop that much of the present-day prosperity is due. The detail in the foreground (opposite page) is, in fact, a representation of the geophysical characteristics of the Gulf of Mexico.

(These pages) the Memphis skyline from Mud Island. Mud Island itself, is a popular entertainment center that revolves around the Mississippi River theme and includes a number of restaurants and varied exhibitions.

(Above) the model on Mud Island, representing the
Mississippi River. (Opposite page) a burning sunset,
seen from Mud Island, gilds the river's surface.
(Overleaf, left) the fountain in the Civic Center
Plaza, Memphis.

During the great flood of 1927, most of Greenville (these pages) remained under water for seventy days. As a result, the Corps of Engineers was called in to close the branch of the Mississippi which entered the city from the north. Today, therefore, Greenville lies on a slack-water arm of the river, the connection to the main channel being to the south. This city in Washington County, Mississippi, is noted for the nearby Winterville Mounds State Park, which is a restoration of the ceremonial gathering place of the Lower Mississippi Valley Indians. The museum there contains many interesting artifacts. For some reason Greenville has also produced a large number of writers, including: William Alexander Percy (who wrote an autobiography relevant to an understanding of the Old South); Walker Percy (winner of the National Book Award) and Hodding Carter (Pulitzer Prize winner for his support of civil rights for blacks), amongst others.

(Above) swampland at Leroy Percy State Park, Washington County. (Opposite page) a sulphurous yellow sun silhouettes the tranquil scene at Lake Chicot State Park, Arkansas, and the only sound comes from the boat which soon passes by and leaves the world to silence.

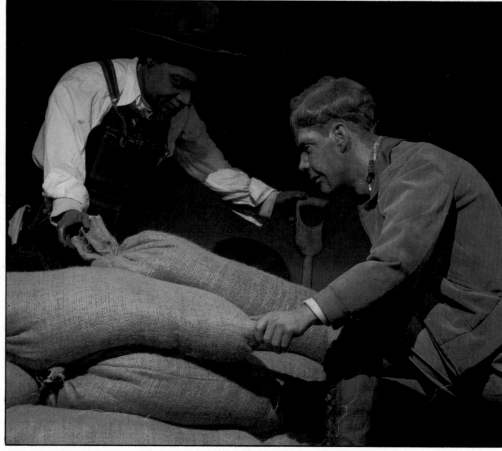

(Previous page and overleaf) the colorful Memphis city scene. (This page) inside the Mud Island River Museum: (above) the bow section of the riverboat replica; (top right) the pilot house and (right) levee workers. (Opposite page) the replica boat within the Schlitz Brewery Hospitality Center.

(Previous page) the statue to Elvis Presley and the Lansky Mural. (This page) to the south of Memphis is Chucalissa, a rebuilt Indian village which had disappeared between de Soto's visit in 1541 and the arrival of Joliet and Marquette in 1673. (Opposite page) mighty bridges span the river.

(Top center) statue of *The Truth Seekers* outside the Cossitt Library. At the courthouse of Shelby County are the statues of *Authority* (left and top left) and *Liberty* (above). (Opposite page) examples of the architectural styles which grace Memphis, whose name means "place of good abode".

Within the Victorian Village area of Memphis are the Fontaine House of 1870 (top left) and (above) the James Lee House of 1848-1871. In Helena, Arkansas, can be found Major James Alexander Tappan House (left) and (opposite page) the Short-Bieri House of 1901.

SHORT-
BIERI
HOUSE 1901

(Above) the vista which unfolds beyond the sun-dappled trees at Beaver Point, in St. Francis National State Park. (Opposite page) the mirror-like surface of Desoto Lake, Coahoma County, Mississippi, reflects the ribbed and fluted tree-trunks which pierce its waters.

(These pages) swampland in Coahoma County, Mississippi.
The lower Mississippi River is, to geographers, in "old
age", looping and twisting over the land in a manner
that led Mark Twain to describe its shape as, "a long,
pliant apple-paring". Swampy backwaters are the result.

Cotton has always been a major crop in Mississippi, as seen (these pages) in Coahoma County. Today, modern machines (opposite page) have taken the back-breaking hardship out of its harvesting. (Above) a farmhand's cottage lies flanked by the fields in which he works.

(These pages) Moon Lake lies to the north of Friars Point in Coahoma County, Mississippi. Subtle shades of pink and peach color the sky and the lake's surface as the sun arcs across the vault of heaven, from dawn (left), to bright day (top) and dusk (remaining pictures).

(Opposite page) the push tug *Coral Dawn* demonstrates its tremendous work capability as it drives a raft of two dozen barges along the broad river's reach. (This page) scenes around Friars Point, Coahoma County, Mississippi. (Below center) the massive, robot-like bulk of a cotton harvesting machine. (Bottom right) the North Delta Museum.

(Opposite page) Desoto Lake, Coahoma County. (This page, top right) the Mississippi River near Friars Point. (Remaining pictures) the Great River Road State Park at Rosedale, Bolivar County: (top left) the observation tower; (above) the banks of the Mississippi; (right) Perry Martin Lake.

(These pages) Vicksburg National Military Park, scene of the 47-day siege of Vicksburg in 1863. President Abraham Lincoln had said, "Vicksburg is the key...The war can never be brought to a close until that key is in our pocket". He knew that without control of the city he would never control the Mississippi and had told General Grant, "...the opening of the Mississippi River will be to us of more advantage than the capture of 40 Richmonds". A Confederate chaplain at the ensuing siege wrote of, "men lying in ditches...under continual fire and on quarter rations...their strength is frittered away". Surrender came on July 4.

EUGENE ERWIN
COL. 6TH MO. C. S. INFTY
KILLED IN BATTLE JUNE 25 1863

MISSISSIPPI

(These pages) the battlefield at Vicksburg, where the men of the Blue and the Gray were swept along inexorably by the red tide of war, clashing amid the roar of cannon and the smoke of musket fire. When Vicksburg surrendered, the Mississippi was lost and the Confederacy was split in half.

HERE BROTHERS FOUGHT FOR THEIR
PRINCIPLES HERE HEROES DIED FOR
THEIR COUNTRY AND A UNITED PEOPLE
WILL FOREVER CHERISH THE PRECIOUS
LEGACY OF THEIR NOBLE MANHOOD

PENNSYLVANIA

(Opposite page, top left) the Old Courthouse, now a museum, was built by slave labor in 1858 and provided an ideal landmark for the ranging of the Union's guns. Thirty-foot columns support its porticos and the clock in the tower is one of the oldest in America. The museum contains a fine collection of Civil War and antebellum Americana. Where the scars left by conflict are still relatively new, the State of Mississippi takes pride in its motto, *Virtute et Armis* (By valor and arms). Vicksburg, itself, always had a tough reputation in its early days. For instance, the first five editors of the *Tri-weekly Sentinel* – established in 1837 – all died violent deaths! (Top center) St. Francis Xavier Convent. (Top right) Levee Street Station. (Bottom pictures) scenes along Washington Street. (This page, right and below) weatherboarded houses in the historic city of Vicksburg. (Far right and bottom right) stern-wheeler on the Yazoo Diversion Canal.

(This page) the Mississippi River Bridges at Vicksburg and the 7.44-inch cannon nicknamed "The Widow Blakeley", which engaged gunboats on May 22, 1863. (Opposite page, top left) Levee Street Station. (Top right and bottom left) the Shirley House. (Bottom right) Cedar Grove, built 1840-58.

(Opposite page) within the darkened depths of bayou country in Warren County, Mississippi. (Right and top left) Lake Washington in Washington County. (Top right) the Mississippi River at Mayersville and (above) Lake Chotard, Issaquena County.

(Left) plaque on the Grand Gulf Historic Tour. (Far left) an old cotton mill near Chatham. (Below) a derelict church at Grand Gulf. (Bottom left) a U.S. Army Wagon of c1900 in the museum in the Grand Gulf Military Monument Park and (opposite page, top left) the Water Mill. (Top right) Stanton Hall, Natchez. Near Port Gibson are the ruins of Windsor (bottom left), which burnt down in 1890. (Bottom right) Auburn, at Duncan Park, Natchez, is a mansion built in 1812 by Levi Weeks.

(These pages) the stately architecture displayed in Natchez, a reminder of days now past. (Top left) historic King's Tavern of 1789. (Above) Connelly's Tavern of 1795, on Ellicott Hill. (Top right) Priest's House. (Right) Rosalie, 1820, was the Federal headquarters during the occupation of Natchez. (Opposite page) beautiful Glen Auburn.

(These pages) elegant Natchez facades: (top left) on Pleasant Hill; (above) along Union Street and (right) Commerce Street. (Top right) magnificent Rosalie. (Opposite page) Longwood, 1858-61, was never completed as intended by its owner, Dr. Haller Nutt, but it is now a National Historic Landmark.

(Top left) palatial Stanton Hall, dating from 1857. (Left and top right) a house on Commerce Street. (Above) the *Southern Lady* at Natchez-under-the-Hill, once a raucous place where, it is said, the only thing cheaper than a woman's body was a man's life. (Opposite page) Baton Rouge from Port Allen.

(Below) the Mississippi River near Natchez. (Left) the West Wing of Jefferson College, Washington. (Bottom left) Myrtle Bank, one of many fine residences surviving in Natchez. (Bottom right and opposite page) the ornate splendor of the drawing room in Stanton Hall, built during the great cotton era using materials and furnishings from Europe.

(These pages) Baton Rouge, Louisiana. (Opposite page) the Old State Capitol of 1847 was burned by a Federal army, but was repaired and served as the State House until 1932. (Right) the Old Arsenal Museum and Park. (Above) the 34-story Louisiana State Capitol. (Top right) the Governor's Mansion.

(Opposite page) riverfront scenes at Baton Rouge. (This page, right) the State Capitol. (Below) driftwood. (Bottom left) the Old Lock House, Plaquemine Locks Commemorative Area. (Bottom right) sugar refinery at White Castle.

(These pages) the Rural Life Museum on the Burden Research Plantation of Louisiana State University. The Museum is a replica – using authentic buildings from surrounding areas – of a typical sugar plantation in the Mississippi Valley. Visitors can see an old schoolhouse, a general store, a blacksmith's workshop and an overseer's cottage. Within a large barn can be seen articles relating to the country life of yesteryear. The University itself was originally established near Alexandria in 1860 and moved to Baton Rouge in 1869. Other museums at the LSU include the Anglo-American Museum in the Memorial Tower, the Geoscience Museum in the Geology Building and the Museum of Natural Science in Foster Hall. The Library contains a collection of the "elephant folio" paintings by Audubon and on the 200-acre campus, which contains some charming lakeside areas, are several Indian mounds dating back over 750 years.

(These pages) The Myrtles, a well-restored St. Francisville plantation of 1796. The long verandah lies shady and cool, trimmed by ornate iron grillwork. The lawn sweeps down to the water's edge and all is quiet, bar the wind soughing among the trees.

(Top left) the Pino House and (left) the Stewart – Dougherty House, Baton Rouge. (Above and opposite page) Oakley House, St. Francisville, is the centerpiece of Audubon Memorial State Park. The plantation home has been furnished as it was in 1821 when John James Audubon (1785-1851), the famous artist and naturalist, lived here. He served as a tutor to the owner's daughter and painted 32 of the birds which appeared in his monumental work, *The Birds of America*, which contained 435 hand-colored plates in 4 volumes.

Plantation homes of the South: (top left) Nottaway Plantation; (left) Oak Alley Plantation, Vacherie; (above and opposite page) Rosedown Plantation, St. Francisville. (Top) Houmas House at Burnside.

There is a startling contrast in New Orleans between
the modern city (above) and the Old Quarter – the
Vieux Carré – which can be viewed in a leisurely
manner from a brightly-painted, horse-drawn carriage
(opposite page).

(Above) at the end of Chartres Street rise the spires
of the Basilica of St. Louis King of France, built in
1794, which was designated a minor basilica by Pope
Paul VI in 1964. (Opposite page) an example of the
ironwork that graces the buildings of the Vieux Carré.

(Previous pages) the explosion of color that marks Mardi Gras in New Orleans. The ornate floats are run by societies called "krewes". The Mystik Krewe of Comus is the earliest known example, having been formed in 1857, with that of Rex (previous pages, left) following in 1872. (These pages and overleaf) mighty sternwheelers ply the Mississippi at New Orleans. The *Natchez* is the ninth riverboat to bear this name, which comes from the Muskogean-speaking Indian tribe that inhabited the east side of the lower Mississippi River. They were sun worshippers, ruled by their monarch – the Great Sun – who held the power of life and death over them. In 1718, Jean Baptiste Le Moyne, Sieur de Bienville, named a new settlement on the Mississippi after the Duc d'Orléans, and New Orleans came into being. In later years, the sight of the bustling trading port prompted Thomas Jefferson to write, "The position of New Orleans certainly destines it to be the greatest city the world has ever seen".

(These pages) the Vieux Carré formed the original area of settlement in New Orleans and remains the cultural heart of the city. (Overleaf, left) Papa Joe's, a well-known eating place. (Overleaf, right) freighters docked at the quayside near to the International Trade Mart.

(These pages) from the clubs and bars of New Orleans, the sound of raucous, lively music filters out to the sidewalks. As you enter, the blare of trumpets fills the air – it's jazz, the greatest musical expression of the South.

(These pages) the stern-wheeler *Natchez* churns through
the waters of the Mississippi River, named by
Algonkian-speaking Indians *Misi* (big) *Sipi* (water).
(Overleaf) the panoramic splendor of New Orleans.
(Page 120) a mansion on St. Charles Avenue.